THE STICKS AND STONES

DIGEST 2018

Shirley J. Davis

Another year has come and gone with the ringing in of January 2019. It has been my privilege to write on my website offering hope to others who are survivors of childhood trauma and who live with dissociative identity disorder.

I had no idea when I began my adventure with a simple blog on WordPress that my website would eventually be read literally all over the globe. It has been a tremendously humbling and deeply satisfying feeling to be allowed to approach subjects that are hard to read and sometimes even harder to write.

This year I would like to dedicate this compilation of the webpages I wrote in 2018 to those others out there who live the realities that accompany surviving horrendous things that should have never happened.

I solute you all and feel honored to bring to you my website and this book containing the highlights of the articles that were published on my site in 2018.

May your journey down the road less taken be rewarding and fruitful.

Shirley J. Davis

The Road Less Taken

The phrase 'the road less taken' was inspired by a beautiful poem written by Robert Frost entitled, 'The Road Not Taken. Although the intention of the poem by Mr. Frost wasn't intended to evoke the strong feelings it does, many people who read it are deeply moved. The Road Less Taken was meant to be a facetious look at his travels around the English countryside, his words say much to the human condition.

We all face decisions that can alter our lives on a regular basis and this poem speaks to many of facing decisions in life and then wondering if we made the correct one. What is we had turned left instead of right? Should we return to where we began and try again?

I Learned Two Things About Myself

When I first read The Road Not Taken, I was inspired because I realized two things about myself.

One, I have made many life-changing decisions, and many of them have been dead ends.

Two, I am not alone in this respect. Everyone makes mistakes in their life decisions. That is totally human and okay.

While thinking on Robert Frost's poem, I thought of how entering and remaining in therapy until finding peace is indeed the road less taken. Therapy is the road that many either choose to avoid or abandon at some point because of the hard and grueling work involved. Those of us who have chosen therapy and to look ourselves straight in the eye, are the exceptions.

So, with that introduction, I am going to attempt to relate my story and show that I'm not just some nut job who claims to have knowledge about dissociative identity disorder, and therapy.

I am shouting out that indeed, I know what I'm talking about.

An Important Note

One important note to my readers.

I have made the decision and promise that on this blog I will not publish any gruesome or highly triggering details. I was sold, used, starved, and a lot of other horrendous things and saying that is enough. Comparing my abuse to yours is useless and I will not promote that line of thinking. Looking to see who suffered more is comparing apples to oranges and doing so is useless and harmful. I do not enjoy playing the one-up-man-ship game, where I you tell me what happened to you and I try to one-up you by telling you something worse. That is childish and very unproductive.

Okay. I will begin the year I was diagnosed and go from there.

From the Beginning

When I was twenty-nine years old, I was working for a huge insurance company, and enjoying my work. I was quickly climbing the corporate ladder and earning more than I ever had before. I knew my childhood was bitter, and I also knew there had been sexual misconduct on the part of a beloved family member. This person had disowned me, but the specifics of what had happened between us were vague.

I didn't consider this vagueness as anything to concern me or the many other abnormalities in my life. These behaviors were things I had lived with all my life and didn't know were different from other people's experiences.

One evening, as I was going to bed, I turned off the light beside my bed. When lay down, I was suddenly no longer in my warm, safe bed, but somewhere else.

I found I had become a little girl, who was being raped. I was screaming and overwhelmed with terror.

The flashback ended abruptly, and I quickly turned the light back on. I had no idea what had just occurred. Shaken, I was afraid to turn the light off again, and spent the rest of the night awake and shivering. I somehow knew it had something to do with my childhood, but I couldn't reconcile what I had just experienced with any firm memories.

These episodes kept happening over and again. They would strike anywhere and at any time, day, night, at work, at home, it didn't seem to make any difference.

A Fateful Night

One evening I was invited by a friend to an incest survivor's group. I had told her of the nightmarish things I had been experiencing, and what little I recalled from my childhood. She suggested I attend her group that night with her.

The following evening, I sat among a group of women survivors not anticipating any insights into what had been happening to me. I hoped to speak to the therapist who led the group after it ended to get her opinion on the strange things that were happening to me.

I Felt Confused

It so happened that night they had a speaker. She got up to tell her story, and I heard maybe two sentences. When I came to myself again I was lying on the floor in the fetal position with the group of women standing protectively around me. I then became aware that the therapist was kneeling beside me speaking in a soothing voice.

I felt confused and afraid. What had just happened? Why were they all looking at me that way?

After the other women had gone home, the therapist sat with me
and we talked. She suggested that I see someone for therapy, but
she felt she was not qualified to help me. She then wrote down
the phone number and address of the therapist who she believed
could help me. It was to be the number of my mentor for almost
three decades who changed my life forever.

The Beginning of My Travels

I walked into Paula's office the first time one day in early
February 1990. I had never been in therapy and had absolutely
no idea what to expect. For the next three months, she sat and
observed me, trying to figure out who I was and just what was
going on with my mind. In discussions many years later, she
related to me how astonished she was by my ability to
consciously leave the room. I would go blank, and she knew that
she was then alone in her office. She pried out of me as much
background as she could and noted the extreme memory gaps
from my childhood. There were many other things that intrigued
her.

Finally, in the spring of 1999, she told me that she believed I
was living with a condition called at that time multiple
personality disorder.

Thus, began our long, hard, almost deadly trip down the road
less taken.

Therapists, the Forgotten Victims of Trauma

I have spent almost thirty years speaking to therapists about the traumatic events that occurred when I was child. When I started out I didn't give the feelings of these brave people much thought. I would expect them to always be available to me. The fact is, many therapists quit their positions as sounding boards, burned out on the horrific stories they hear, and the frustrating efforts they make to help traumatized people out of the abyss.

They are the forgotten victims of trauma.

This article is written to help bring to light what therapists go through listening as they do to severely traumatized clients for eight or more hours a day, four or five days a week, year after year.

Can You Walk in Their Shoes?

Suppose you are a therapist and you are seeing a client who was severely traumatized in childhood. The client enters your care but doesn't trust you. Everything you suggest, and all your training can't change anyone else, but you do your best to help this client see reality as much as possible. You invest a lot of your own mental power into this person and hope to hell they will not only get better but will survive.

You sit with this horribly injured person once or twice a week and listen to the stories of what they went through. You have young children of your own, and the thought of them being injured the way this client was stirs your heart. You are only human, and the feelings of anger and intense sadness you feel can be overwhelming. You weep openly before your client when told some of the things that were done to them at such a young age, but your client doesn't weep with you. They are out of tune with the emotions that they should be feeling when they tell these horror stories. This must be so lonely.

Therapists Face Hardships

Can you imagine the emotional strain on that therapist? Can you feel at all the frustration they must feel? How can they disconnect from an intense session where the client relates to them the tragedy that was their childhood?

Even the best trained and most dedicated therapists have limits. They are, as I already stated, only human. They have a life outside the office, they have families, they have children and go to church. Yet, they are dedicated to helping their clients find peace.

It Must Be Very Straining

Then there the clients who don't survive. It is an unfortunate fact that 20-30% therapists will have a client commit suicide during the time they are being treated.

I had a therapist who had this happen to her. The day her client died she came to my apartment to follow through with an appointment even though she had just received news that one of her clients had died at their own hand. I knew immediately something was wrong as she was totally distracted and on the verge of tears. Finally, I stopped our discussion and point blank asked her what was wrong and what had happened. She began to weep and told me she had lost a client to suicide. I sent her home. I knew she was overwrought and was shocked that she hadn't cancelled out appointment after receiving such news.

She was so dedicated to helping me that she chose to sacrifice
her own mental health and her need to grieve, to see me. That
wasn't a healthy choice, not at all, but she felt keeping our
appointment was that important.

The Price They Pay to Help is Very High

The rate of divorce for therapists is much higher than the general
population. One can see why. If you were married to a person
who returns home each evening mentally exhausted but unable
to tell you why, how would you feel? They are distant, tired and
only partially connected to what is happening at home because
they are mentally trying to leave work at work but finding it
almost impossible.

Therapists are People First.

They can't simply turn off their emotions after seeing a client.
The best training does not prepare you enough for the strong
emotions you feel when confronted with highly traumatized
clients.

If a client sees a therapist for an extended time, say for years, the
therapist and the client form a bond that isn't easily broken. It
isn't friendship, that isn't what a therapist is, but perhaps
something even deeper. Then one day the client that you have
invested so much of your time and emotions in disappears. They
suddenly quit showing up for appointments and you never hear
from them again.

I had been seeing my first therapist Paula for over seven years
when my husband became ill and we had to take bankruptcy. I
went to my next appointment after our court appearance but was
told by the business office that I could not see Paula. Not even to
say goodbye.

Years later, fifteen to be exact, I returned to Paula's office. We had a joyful reunion but later after I had told her what had occurred, she told me she thought I had become angry with her and quit. The clinic had not told her the reason for my not returning to her office. I could tell when she related these thoughts that my sudden disappearance after so many years had caused her pain. I will never know exactly how much because she was much too professional to relate that, but I had a deep attachment to her, and I refuse to believe those feelings weren't reciprocated.

God, that must have been so hard!

Vacations are Vital

When I began therapy I would become furious at my therapists when they took a vacation. How dare they leave me and not be available should I need them! Only later did I understand that vacations are critical for a therapist's mental health and their ability to help their clients. It's a time to reflect and regroup. It's also a time to mend their relationships with their families.

My hat is off, and my respect given to the brave men and women who work as therapists. They sacrifice so much yet are very careful not to let their clients know the strain their speaking about their lives is causing. They care and that is the biggest and hardest thing of all.

Try to Remember

The next time your therapist is ill and calls in sick or the clinic calls you to cancel an appointment because they will not be in without an explanation, try to remember. Please, try to remember they are people first and that their absence in no way reflects on how they feel about you.

Therapists are indeed the forgotten victims of trauma. Their lives, their relationships, and their mental health all suffer the grief and pain they hear from the people of which they have grown fond. They grow fond of clients that they see often and feel their pain and sorrow. Yet, they are forced to separate themselves from the horror stories they hear and attempt to leave it at work.

I cannot imagine the strength it must take not to leave the listening profession.

Yes, Therapists are the Forgotten Victims of Trauma.

"The shock of any trauma, I think changes your life. It's more acute in the beginning and after a little time, you settle back to what you were. However, it leaves an indelible mark on your psyche." Alex Lifeson

I Refuse to Be Defined by Trauma

One thing I know I do not want in my future is to be defined by the history I have in therapy and trauma. It is a part of who I am, but it isn't all I am. I don't want people to feel sorry for me or to doubt my abilities because of what I have been through these past fifty-seven years of life.

Will I Tell People in the Future About My Past?

Maybe. Maybe not. It all depends on who they are and why they need to know about it. I cannot in all good conscience leave a person suffering alone without telling them I understand their pain, but I am not going to seek out situations where I need not tell my story anymore. At least not until I am firmly established as a Scientist on my merits and my ability to contribute to the world.

How I Want to be Seen

I want my future bosses to see me as Shirley Davis Ph.D. who is an excellent Scientist with many ideas that are worth pursuing. I don't want them to not see me as Shirley Davis Ph.D. the poor thing who lived through hell and deserves our pity.

I once thought that way but no more. It's a stage everyone goes through, wanting people to feel sorry for you, but I am a force to be reckoned with like Superman and I don't expect people to pity me.

I expect to be challenged by my superiors, for them to ask me the hard questions that need answered. I expect them to treat me like anyone else they have trained or hired.

I expect to live life in the open, unashamed but not telling everyone my past as though it were a badge I must wear. There is a huge amount of head rush involved in knowing I have outlived my abusers, but I am choosing not to be defined by my past any longer. I have chosen not to live under the umbrella of "abuse victim" I have chosen instead to be known as a "conqueror and life-changer."

Do You Understand What I Am Trying to Say?

I hope so.

There are many, many people whom I have had the privilege to know who will never move beyond their diagnosis. When I ask why they are choosing to remain stuck in the trauma they are working so hard to escape from, they often react in anger and either shut themselves off from me or decide I am trying to harm them. The reason? Because I dare to ask the hard questions that challenge their self-beliefs. However, they forget, I've been where they are, and I understand their pain. The questions I ask aren't to harm them, but to help them see there is a better life than deciding to live forever in the absolute hell of the past. Their words hurt, but still, I choose not to define myself by them.

Who I Truly Am

The experiences and challenges I have conquered are, to be sure, something to be proud of but I am to move on with my life.

Realistically I understand that I am forever changed by the trauma of the past. However, as I said in the beginning of this piece, that is only a part of who I am. Shirley J. Davis is a warm, considerate, intelligent, and caring person. She is a public speaker, a freelance writer, an international blogger, and many other things. Most of all, she is someone who wants to help.

Yet the best description of all, and the one that describes me the best is that despite all the trauma and horror of my past, I am undefined by it.

I am undefined.

"Your only identity is I AM undefined and infinite. Any label you give yourself limits yourself." Deepak Chopra

It's Time for Therapist's to Reexamine Their Thoughts on Their Client's Ability to Get Well

I attended a function last weekend and heard some marvellous speakers. They told their stories of recovery from severe mental health issues. While listening to them speak, I was reminded of something. I have written about this topic before, but it needs to be reiterated over and again. This theme needs to be desperately heard by those who treat any type of mental health problem, and especially something as exacerbating as Dissociative Identity Disorder.

People in treatment for any type of mental disorder or disability excel when their therapist believes they WILL get well.

The Miracle of Life-Giving Recovery

That may sound like a simple statement, but it is full of meaning. When a therapist believes their patient is going to get well, they exude the confidence and hope that their clients need.

One must remember that people living with DID have been severely betrayed and are very ill. They need hope and care. When they encounter a therapist, who shows them in both verbal and non-verbal languages that they believe in their ability to get well, the miracle of lifegiving recovery.

However, the Converse is True

If someone walks into a therapist's office with DID and your belief is they will never, ever get well, it is written all over you. Oh, the words may not be spoken, and you may placate that client, but they won't heal. They will only get well exactly as much as you feel they can, and if you don't believe they will heal, they will not.

Why is this?

Humans are social animals, and we depend on each other for all kinds of support, including emotional. We are also very intuitive. We can sense whether another person likes us or believes in us. We all do it without thinking about it. We form our self-beliefs quite a bit on what we believe others feel about us from verbal and non-verbal cues.

So, all too often when a client enters a therapist's office suffering from the symptoms of living with DID they are usually desperately looking for help. They need acceptance and hope not someone thinking to themselves "He/she is a hopeless case".

I Know I'm Being Too Harsh

I have had personal experience with both types of therapists. My first therapist was very supportive and did not doubt for a moment I was going to get well. If she did, she was very good at hiding it. She was tirelessly dedicated to finding ways to help me deal with my symptoms, and ways to help bring them under control.

However, after I lost her for a while I fell into the care of several therapists who were wholeheartedly the opposite. I felt so lost and alone, then began to quickly decline until I was placed inpatient where I lived for over seven years. One of my therapists told my family that I was totally hopeless case, and that's how it felt.

What?

If a therapist doesn't know or want to treat a client, they should not accept them even for the first appointment and be honest with them. A therapist should never be afraid to admit to themselves they aren't qualified to treat someone, or be afraid to say the magic words, "I don't know".

Now, I realize there is very little training available on how to treat DID, but my first therapist didn't know either.

How Did My First Therapist Do It?

My therapist flew by the seat of her pants and called enormously on her training, but SHE NEVER, EVER GAVE UP! She never thought to herself or said to me in any physical or verbal fashion that I was hopeless and a waste of her time. Yes, she did employ some very tough tactics when I acted childishly or got stuck in my own misery, but she always was my rock.

She was the one person I knew was going to be there.

I knew she believed in me.

Her belief and solidarity made all the difference in the world.

I am now functioning very well and living an average and very successful life. All because someone believed that I would.

More Therapists Need to Believe in Their Clients

The state of Illinois has a slogan, "The Expectation is Recovery". Providers all over the world need to reconsider their thoughts on the clients they treat and align themselves with this motto.

Perhaps You Should Re-examine the Reasons You Entered the Listening Profession.

Did you get in it for the money? I hope no. There isn't much to be earned.

Did you get in it for prestige? I hope not, there isn't much prestige in being someone who sits in an office and listens to people's problems all day.

Did you get into the listening profession because you thought it was easy? I hope not. Being a counsellor must be one of the toughest and most draining jobs in the world.

Or

Did you get into it to help people overcome their psychiatric difficulties and learn to live healthy happy lives? I hope so. This is the noblest profession, helping others.

No One is Hopeless, All People Are Valuable

I didn't write this piece to tell people off. I wrote it to reiterate what many people hopefully already know. People who enter a therapist's office ARE NOT hopeless cases and are valuable human beings.

No matter what their diagnosis.

"As human beings, our job in life is to help people realize how rare and valuable each one of us really is, and that each of us has something that no one else has or ever will have—something inside that is unique to all time. It's our job to encourage uniqueness and to provide ways of developing its expression."

~ Fred Rogers

The Awesome Power of Words

An old adage that states, "Sticks and stones may break my bones, but words will never hurt me."

That's not true.

What we say to ourselves and about ourselves to others can and does harm us.

I recently attended an event where I listened to folks who have lived experience with internal controversies, what some would term mental illnesses. One of these marvellous speakers was Nanette Larson, a personal hero of mine and many others here in Illinois. She has, like all humans, struggled hard to find her niche in the world and has a loud voice in the mental health system of my state.

Out of all the remarkable things she spoke about that Saturday afternoon one has stuck in my mind, the importance of language.

How Describing Oneself Is Important

Everyone is familiar with how using words to describe a person's color is looked down on by today's society. An African-American person is horribly disturbed, and rightly so, when called the N word. Yet, I've heard it used on television by African-Americans to describe themselves.

You may wonder, what is wrong with that? Don't they have that right? Of course. Everyone should have the right speak as they wish if they don't interfere with someone else's life. However, if saying the N word is considered harmful when used by someone else when speaking isn't it harmful to use it to describe oneself?

Yes. Why?

The N word is linked to being degraded and dehumanized. It is a word that says you are owned and worthless. Calling oneself the N word is saying to yourself and to others that you relate yourself to that title.

Think about that.

You are saying not only to anyone else you may meet but to yourself that you believe you are a worthless piece of chattel instead of a worthwhile and necessary part of humanity.

History Can Teach a Lot About the Power of Words

An extreme case and point came from the hideous abuse of words used by Nazi Germany. Joseph Goebbels used the human tendency to follow a crowd and humanities seemingly endless desire to be better than others against his own people. He was very careful to structure and use words to persuade the people of Germany who they should see as "acceptable" people. The Nazi party spent a lot of time and money describing the people they chose as Aryans, pure and demonizing everyone else.

They wanted people who did not fit their criteria to been seen by labels only. They convinced the people, through propaganda, that anyone who did not match their strict vision of what humanity should be were not worthy of life. This meant millions of men, women and children were non-contributing users living off the government and thus the taxpayer's money.

Sound eerily familiar?

Although I do not believe the people who were murdered ever thought of themselves as worthless, the population of Germany came to that conclusion. They actively and passively took part in the slaughter of millions in a systematic murder of millions of innocent people.

While that may seem like an extreme example, is it really? Things like this still go on in our world today in countries all over the world. Even here in the United States, a land of abundant resources people like me, who are unable to work and must draw social security and/or use food stamps are labelled users, takers and not valuable. Is less than human next? Food for thought.

Yes, Words Can Be Deadly

Calling oneself mentally ill or saying you suffer with a mental illness also labels you. This title says to yourself and society that you are hopelessly unstable, untrustworthy and sick. It also states that you feel sorry for yourself and most importantly of all will never get well.

Poppycock

As I have said in other pieces, I was diagnosed in 1990 with dissociative identity disorder, a severe brain dysfunction. At one time I described myself as suffering with this condition and being very sick. Not only this, I called myself a victim of my past. Inevitably when I told people about my diagnosis their reactions weren't good. Some pitied me, some stopped being my friends and yet others feared me. I even had a woman who had trusted me around her children suddenly avoid me after I told her about my diagnosis.

Who Am I Really?

I no longer say I am suffering, ill, or a victim, I now say I live with a condition known as dissociative identity disorder caused by severe childhood trauma. I realize they sound similar, but the difference in the way I see myself and how others see me is enormous.

I'm Living, Not Suffering. I've climbed out of the suffering mentality and into the living one. I no longer see myself as being controlled by my brain disorder, I see it as the best thing that has ever happened to me. It has made me more loving, understanding and able to help the world than not living with it ever would have done.

I had someone on a social media site once ask me in a not so nice way if I lived with a man called DID. I very nicely answered no, but I am alive and DID is only a part of who I am.

I'm Not Ill. By calling myself mentally ill I am saying that I am sick and to others this may mean contagious. Some even see illnesses as being incurable or fatal. When I call myself mentally ill I am saying to myself I will never get well.

Yes, I live a very complex life sometimes due to the symptoms of dissociative identity disorder, but I am not sick. I live with diabetes and have high blood pressure too, but these problems don't mean I'm ill. These are just conditions that are part of my life which are treatable. This is also true of DID.

Am I a Victim? Maybe I when I was a helpless child, but no longer. The only one who can hurt me and keep me from being happy today is me. Calling myself a victim of childhood trauma is saying that I am still under the control of those who harmed me. That simply is not true.

Am I A Consumer? Perhaps the term that disturbs me the most is when I am termed a consumer. People who receive services from the mental health system are called this term, but why? What am I consuming?

According to the website, Dictionary.com the word consuming means "to destroy and to use up."

What am I destroying and using up? I a therapist and take medication to treat my symptoms, but how am I destroying or using up anything that others with types of disorders?

No One Brought Me a Casserole

True, DID is a chronic and lifelong disorder, but so is diabetes. Yet there is no one who considers the millions of people who live with diabetes users and takers.

What about cancer? I know from first-hand experience that cancer is a very expensive disease and when you are going through the surgery and treatments you need help. A person can't go to the store without seeing a canister on the counter asking for funds to help a cancer patient pay his rent and other expenses. Dinners and other functions are held to support people with cancer, and neighbours bring over casseroles.

It's Time for a Change

Yet, if are diagnosed and going through treatment for a severe bout of depression or have a child who has developed the symptoms of schizophrenia no one comes rushing to your aid. In fact, you are more likely to be shunned.

How do people often measure the worth of another human being? Words.

For far too long society has used words to devalue other human beings. It's time for a change.

Where Does It Begin?

It begins with changing the way we use words in our self-talk. It starts by saying to ourselves that we are not worthless consumers, nor are we a waste of space. We are worthwhile human beings with hopes, desires and dreams.

As you can see, words are very powerful. They shape the way we see ourselves and how others see us. I urge all of you to make a list of all your good points. If you are having a bad day, start small. Do you have pretty eyes? Are you a good friend? Do you love animals?

Everyone, and I mean EVERYONE have abilities and good points.

What you say to yourself today will change your attitude about yourself and in that way, help change the world.

Below is only one resource available online. All you need to do is google it and you will find tons of ways to change yourself. Together we can end stigma by using the awesome power of words.

"Words have energy and power with the ability to help, to heal, to hinder, to hurt, to harm, to humiliate, and to humble." -Yehuda Berg

Who Is to Blame?

In the wake of the school shootings and stabbings, people are trying to come to terms with a society that would allow and carry out such crimes. In the process, many are starting to play the blame game, and one of the unfortunate victims have become the mentally ill.

I understand the thinking and the political motivations. That's why I am writing this piece. I'm not going to try to blame any one person or entity for these unfortunate turn of events but I am going to offer some sobering information from the point of view of someone who has lived with severe mental illness all her life.

Victim or Perpetrator

It is a fact that in any demographic (sex, sexual orientation, occupation, urban, suburban, etc.) there are those who would commit violence against others. Approximately 2% of people living with a mental illness will do so, no greater and no less than any other group. People who live with mental illness are far more likely to become victims of violent crime than the perpetrators of it.

That having been said, it may be true that the people who have committed mass murder in our schools, churches and at concerts here in the United States may have lived with a mental condition. However, they were undiagnosed and in the cases of the children, were ignored. The kids who shot up the Columbine High School were known to be unstable, as was the teen in Florida, yet with all the evidence sitting right in front of all, it was ignored.

Why? What Is Wrong?

One problem, and perhaps it all, stems from stigma.

Stigma is a potent influence in our society. For hundreds if not for thousands of years, being diagnosed with a mental health condition has been considered a life sentence. Even with the advancements we now have in science, people who have themselves or have a relative who has such a diagnosis are shunned and shut out.

Until the Obama administration, even medical insurance denied paying for care for mental health conditions even though the costs and prognosis for those living with them were much lower and better than other physical diseases such as cancer or diabetes.

Stigma is Powerful

I have had to leave two houses of worship not because I acted strangely or caused a disruption, but because once the people found out I had a mental health condition, they became afraid of me. Some even refused to sit in the same pew as I did. These people aren't evil folks, just people who don't understand and do not care to find out the facts.

Isn't the biggest culprit here? People being afraid to face the facts? Are we so terrified of looking at the truth that we would sacrifice the lives of innocent men, women, and children?

Few Sobering Things to Think About

Here are just a few sobering facts to ponder.

The father of one of the Columbine shooters had been notified several times by the police and the high school that his son had done disturbing, and in a few instances, illegal things. The father's answer? "My son is a victim. He did nothing wrong." Here it was clearly not only a lack of taking responsibility but being fearful of stigma.

Columbine was aware of the strange behaviours of the two youths who were to later kill themselves and several innocents. They either could not or would not act.

Our politicians in Washington are terrified of losing their positions of power and authority, so they turn the other way and do nothing when faced with the hatred and fear in our country. This isn't just recently, this has been going on for decades. They have forgotten who they are supposed to be working for, the American people.

The youth who killed so many in Florida recently also had been noticed by his school. He had been, at one time, denied carrying a backpack to school for fear it might be hiding weapons. Finally, he was expelled. The local police and the FBI knew about him but did nothing. People were afraid to act.

There are currently very few and in some instances no counsellors in our schools. Those who are have been hampered by the bureaucracy and red tape involved in helping kids. They are left powerless to act on behalf of troubled kids, and like myself, their pain and suffering go untreated.

Child and family services are so tied up with cases they can prove to involve child abuse that many of our children fall through the cracks. The reason? No one wants to fund them. They are on the number one hit list of cost-slashing in many states. It's as though the United States values their children so lowly that raising property taxes or doing anything to help our kids gets easily marked off.

The media is helping to perpetuate the problem. I understand that people have the right to know about these horrible events, but to carelessly report such things is to engender a type of immortality to the killers. The scenes are not just reported once or when necessary, they are played over and over again. This reporting invites other lonely or disenfranchised youths and adults to think about how they too can reach a place in history by doing the same.

The Answers Aren't Easy

I fully understand that the answers to these problems aren't easy, and to be frank, many people will have their toes stepped finding them. But blaming the mentally ill, the gun owners, or the politicians alone will not solve anything.

We must work together. That means sitting down and taking a hard look at all our attitudes. Try to find out why so many of our kids are turning into mass murders.

We need to come together like never before as a nation, as a people, with open, honest dialogue.

We must stop acting like toddlers and end the finger-pointing.

Who is To Blame?

Who killed those children at Columbine and in Florida?

We all did. Every one of us.

The Deep Abyss Called Depression

I have spent a great deal of time on this blog and elsewhere
talking about my recovery and how I live in relative peace with
my alters. What I haven't discussed is my co-occurring
diagnosis of major depression.

A Double Whammy

It is not unusual for people who have been victims of severe
childhood trauma to experience depression. Lord knows it has
cost enough lives. I've had depressive symptoms since I was at
least seven, and perhaps younger. My paediatrician began
treating me for depressive symptoms when I was six with the
only drug available at that time, Phenobarbital. One month
before my seventh birthday I attempted suicide. Yes, depression
has killed many, many good people.

So, I live with the double whammy of major depression and
dissociative identity disorder.

Pure Hell

What does it feel like live with both these debilitating disorders?

It feels like pure hell.

Getting up in the morning feels like you are pulling yourself up a
steep cliff with no rope. You can't speak with anyone, and if you

do you are not civil. You ache all over your body and feel dark
and alone.

If you are like me and live with DID, the symptoms of that
diagnosis can become worse. I experience more lost time and
disorientation. I have a very hard time keeping track of the day
and even the year.

I do not feel like this all the time anymore. As I have already
stated, most of the time my depression is under control, but there
is a certain time of the year when I fall into a deep, dark hole.
This has gone on my entire life.

There Is A Pattern

For many years I didn't understand the pattern. Then last year I
began seeing a new therapist and psychiatrist who began to look
at my records and they noticed a pattern that I had been totally
unaware of, I would fall into the abyss in the spring.

Now that may seem counterintuitive. Aren't the spring months
when people begin to feel better not worse?

My therapist challenged me to make a list of major events that
occurred between March and July in my life. To my amazement
the list was long and they all seemed to have occurred in the
spring. There were many deaths, sicknesses and other things that
had occurred in spring throughout my life.

Ammunition

When I showed my list to my therapist at my next visit, she
shared it with my psychiatrist. His first words were, "Now we
have ammunition to fight with." What he meant was we could
begin in late February or early March to increase my
antidepressant medication to ward off the increase of depression
that was sure to come.

This morning I awoke feeling horrible. I am depressed and moody. It's time for me to see my psychiatrist.

My Point

I guess the point I wanted to make with this entry is that depression, even when it is founded in severe trauma, does not have to be a death sentence or ruin your life.

Even if you also live with DID. There are no magic pills, but the correct antidepressant can help enormously.

Genetic Testing

One thing I wanted to make my readers aware of is the genetic testing that can now be done to find out which medications will work best with your body. These tests are available to psychiatrists, and Medicare and Medicaid will pay for them if your doctor gives a qualifying diagnosis. They swab the inside of your cheeks, then mail the swabs to a lab. Within a few days you get the results. When I received my results, they said that many of the drugs I had taken in the past were contraindicated for my body makeup. The list of things that would help was only three drugs long.

However, now that we know what drugs work best, my Psychiatrist has ordered me one of them and not surprisingly, I feel better.

If you are on Medicaid or Medicare, ask your doctor to test you. It can mean the difference between stumbling around from drug to drug and finding one that works.

"You shall be free indeed when your days are not without a care nor your nights without want and a grief. But rather when these things girdle your life and yet you rise above them naked and unbound." – Khalil Gibran

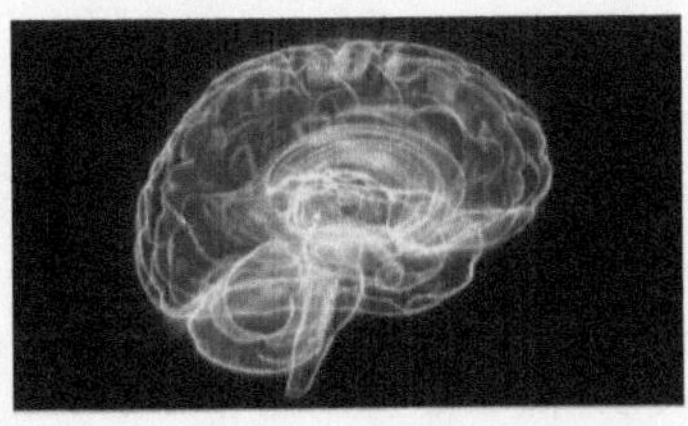

Brain Anatomy in Brief

A brief description of brain anatomy is in order.

The brain is split into two hemispheres, the right, and the left. Under normal circumstances, these two parts of the brain mirror one another and things that happen on one side of the body is processed in the opposite hemisphere.

For these two parts of your brain to communicate, there is a complex region called the corpus callosum. This area can be described as a collection of organic wiring which is covered by a fatty layer which acts as insulation like an electric wire. Like an electric wire, the wiring functions well only with this protective coating of insulation and without it or without enough of it, a short can occur which keeps the signals from either passing through well or at all.

There has been ample research to see what can occur if this wiring is missing using by studying people who have had to have their corpus callosum cut to stop seizures in severe epilepsy.

What They Found Is Amazing

The left hemisphere, it has been found, acts as an interpreter of what is going on in our world, where the right hemisphere is the mute partner that comprehends our environment.

In other words, the right hemisphere understands what is going on but cannot elaborate other than to act, and the left interprets why that action occurred.

For example, a person with a split brain sits in a chair with headphones on. They are told in their right ear (right hemisphere) to stand up, walk across a room, and pick up a pencil. Immediately they will rise and do the task they were asked to do. When the person is then asked why they did the action, their left hemisphere makes up a story because it has no clue. It may state, "I wanted to." Or "I needed a pencil." The person who is being tested will not know they have lied, in fact to them what they said is exactly what happened.

A Correlation?

Everyone is familiar with the idea that if an electric wire loses its insulation, it will short out and not carry a current. The same can be said of the corpus callosum.

So, when my neuroscience class in college covered a chapter on the corpus callosum and its importance to helping the brain hemispheres "speak" to one another, with emphasis on the importance of myelin (the fatty tissue) that acts as insulation on the "wiring," I began to suspect there may be a correlation between a commonly reported symptom of Borderline Personality Disorder, mythomania (clinical term pseudologia fantastica).

Mythomania

Mythomania is a very difficult and frustrating symptom that is very hard to treat. The person who exhibits this symptom tells lies and believes them to be true. No amount of persuasion can dissuade them from their beliefs and they often feel persecuted and ill-used when confronted with their fabrications.

I asked myself the question, have there been studies done on changes to the corpus callosum in people living with borderline personality disorder? I began to search, and I found tons of research.

Normal Formation of the Corpus Callosum

Under usual circumstances, the human brain of a child experiences an amazing growth between the ages of birth to seventeen years of age. White matter (the corpus callosum included) increases rapidly as the grey matter (the other structures) decrease. However, the size of the brain does not change.

With positive and stimulating input from experiences in their environment, children's "wiring" between the two hemispheres develops healthy myelination (coating by fatty insulation) and the child can regulate well their emotions and integrate their experiences normally.

The Effects of Childhood Trauma

However, if there is intense stress in the child's life, such that the stress hormones involved in activating the fight, flight or flee response continually blood the child's brain, the myelin coating (insulation) on the corpus callosum does form correctly.

What I am saying is that a child's brain can be severely damaged by overwhelming stressful situations such as abuse and neglect. In these situations, children aren't allowed to go back to the baseline after being afraid, and the hormones that their bodies have released are toxic to normal brain development. They experience brain damage.

What is My Point?

I have considered my experiences with folks who have been
diagnosed with Borderline Personality Disorder and how they
would hear or see something experienced by someone else and
within a few days to hours believe they are also experiencing the
same thing.

What I am saying is that they use mythomania to describe their
experiences when interacting with their environment.

For example, a person living with borderline personality
disorder hears on television there is a nasty flu bug going around
complete with the symptoms being suffered by those unfortunate
enough to contract it.

Within hours or days of hearing this news, they too believe they
are ill even though do not actually have the flu.

This is only one mild example of the kind of effects of
mythomania. The idea that they have the flu isn't something
they are lying about, they sincerely believe they are afflicted
with the disorder and will act on those beliefs.

This behaviour sounds a lot to me like the right hemisphere
hearing something, and the left hemisphere misinterpreting what
was said and making up a story to explain the behaviour.

What the Research Shows

I found research done using fMRI (functional magnetic
resonance imaging) done on people with Borderline Personality
Disorder. There in black and white before my eyes was proof
that yes, the myelin insulation had been found to be damaged.
This means that signals from one hemisphere of the brain are not
efficiently transduced (electrically connected) to the other.

These findings aren't just for borderline personality disorder, but
for schizophrenia, bipolar disorder and many other mentally
challenging disorders.

My Theory About What is Happening

The extreme stress experienced by children in childhood trauma floods their young developing brains with hormones that cause them not to be able to properly form myelin sheaths around the neurons that make up the corpus callosum.

The result is that the left hemisphere and right hemisphere lose the ability to communicate efficiently. Thus mythomania (pseudologia fantastica), visual and audio hallucinations and a host of other mental health problems form and inhibit people from having ordinary lives.

My Plea and My Hope

My sincere hope is that someone with a Ph.D. who is involved in research may consider this post and begin a new program.

What if I am right? What is the damage done to the corpus callosum during childhood is the basis for many of the major mental illnesses that have been recognized including Schizophrenia, Bipolar Disorder, Borderline Personality Disorder, Alzheimer's Disease and Dissociative Identity Disorder?

Shouldn't the mental health field be coupling with the folks who are at the forefront of research being done to treat and possibly cure Multiple Sclerosis, a disorder known to involve the myelination of the brain?

There is a Cure on the Horizon!

There are great advances being done right now in laboratories around the world in genetics and its uses to replace damaged parts of the body. Can the corpus callosum be one of these damaged organs that is replaced in the future?

That would mean cures for many if not of the major mental disabilities known today.

What if?

Think about it.

"The power of one, if fearless and focused, is formidable, but the power of many working together is better." Gloria Macapagal Arroyo

References

Below are only a few of the papers I have found about research being done on the corpus callosum and mental health.

Dodja, A., Sesar, K., & Simiae, N., (2018). The Neurobiological Aspects of Exposure to

Childhood Maltreatment. In Costa, A., & Villaba, E. (Ed.), Horizons in Neuroscience

Research (Volume 35, Ch. 3). Zadar, Croatia: Nova Biomedical

https://www.novapublishers.com/catalog/product_info.php?products_id=64102The neuroendocrinological sequelae of stress during brain development: the impact of child abuse and neglect

A Panzer - African journal of psychiatry, 2008 - journals.co.za

… to glucose depletion in the hippocampal cells, making them sensitive to **damage** by **excess**
glutamate.7 … 3 Oligodendrocytes make the **myelin sheaths** of neurons, ie white matter.16 **High**
levels of … superior temporal gyrus3, or it may be the basis of the **increased** social intelligence …

Introduction to the special section: myelin and
oligodendrocyte abnormalities in schizophrenia

V Haroutunian, KL Davis -
… of **Neuropsychopharmacology**, **2007** - academic.oup.com…
International **Journal** of **Neuropsychopharmacology**. **Published online: 12 February 2007**
…
Futher evidence for altered myelin biosynthesis and
glutamatergic dysfunction in
schizophrenia.
International **Journal** of **Neuropsychopharmacology** …

The neuroendocrinological sequelae of stress during brain
development: the impact of child abuse and neglect

A Panzer - African journal of psychiatry, 2008 - journals.co.za

Severe stress during the sensitive periods of neurodevelopment,
(which include the prenatal period, infancy, childhood and
adolescence), has a long-lasting organizing effect on the brain
and stress axes. Child abuse and neglect thus exert a cumulative
harmful effect on neuroendocrinological development, which
persists into adulthood. It is not merely the memory of the
trauma which leaves a mark, but rather the effect on
neurodevelopment which negatively influences the ability of
adult survivors of childhood maltreatment to cope with

Social experience-dependent myelination: an implication
for psychiatric disorders

M Toritsuka, M Makinodan, T Kishimoto - Neural plasticity,
2015 - hindawi.com

Myelination is one of the strategies to promote the conduction
velocity of axons in order to adjust to evolving environment in
vertebrates. It has been shown that myelin formation depends on

genetic programming and experience, including multiple factors, intracellular and extracellular molecules, and neuronal activities. Recently, accumulating studies have shown that myelination in the central nervous system changes more dynamically in response to neuronal activities and experience than expected.

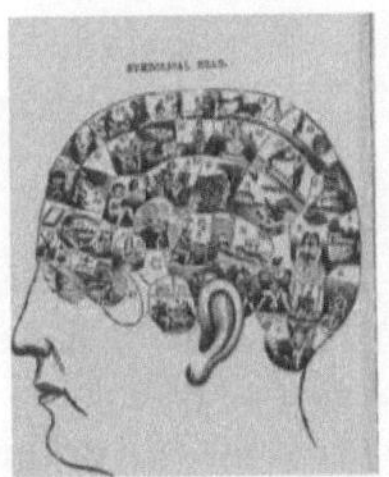

Traumatic Memory Retrieval and Dissociative Identity Disorder

Suddenly beginning to remember traumatic events from childhood is a hallmark of dissociative identity disorder. Have you ever researched to find out why this is so? I have, and my findings thus far are intriguing. This piece is another branch of the research I have already done on the corpus callosum, the wiring of our brains, but it goes a bit farther.

The Corpus Callosum

One of these things is the importance of the corpus callosum in the regulation, overall function, and health of the brain. This a region deep in the brain that consists of bundles of nerves that acts like wiring connecting the two sides of our minds. Without going too deeply, these wires cannot work correctly if the myelin, a fatty substance that coats them, is damaged or does not form properly.

There are many reasons and diseases associated with damage to the corpus callosum including and most important for our purposes here, chronic traumatic stress. When a child's brain is flooded with the hormones that are secreted to make the body ready for the fight, flight or freeze response when danger is perceived have horrible side effects if the child can never return to baseline levels.

In other words, if the child continues to feel threatened 24/7 and year after year their little brains are incapable of getting a rest from these vital substances. Over time many of the structures of the brain are damaged including the amygdala, hippocampus and corpus callosum.

There is a significant substance that coats the "wiring" of the corpus callosum called myelin that acts like insulation. Just like with electrical wiring in your home, if the insulation is broken or missing the wiring cannot propagate a signal correctly or may short out. Chronic stress in early childhood prevents the brain from achieving full myelination, decreasing the connectiveness between the two hemispheres of the brain.

Hang on to Your Hats

What follows next in this piece will put together many of the pieces of the puzzle I have been missing for so long.

I have uncovered research that explains why people who live with DID or any other dissociative or severe mental illness report they cannot remember their childhood abuse until later in life. This research is scattered here and there among the many scientific papers on the Internet, and that is probably why no one until now has pulled it all together.

Brain Structures Called Ventricles

There are structures in the brain known as ventricles which contain cerebral spinal fluid (CSF). Made up of four primary structures, the lateral ventricle is the one which caught my attention. It is here (and a few other places as well) in the choroid plexus that the cerebral spinal fluid is manufactured.

CFS is vital to the working of our brains, as it circulates and removes the waste products produced in metabolism by the brain cells kind of like the way our intestinal system and kidneys remove waste products from our body. Without this circulation, our brains would become overwhelmed with waste and would die. Interestingly what has many structures of the brain that can be affected, the corpus callosum is one of the first to be changed. A breakdown of the circulation of CFS will cause it to thin and shrink.

Thinning and shrinking of the corpus callosum means that the wiring between the two hemispheres becomes inefficient and thus there is a breakdown of communication between them.

I believe this is the basis of many major psychiatric disorders such as borderline personality disorder, bipolar disorder, schizophrenia and major depression.

What's That Got to Do with Anything?

Okay, you may be thinking, but what about suddenly remembering traumatic memories from childhood?

The number of fibres (wires), in the corpus callosum are fixed at birth. However, they grow thicker and thinner in different stages of life. These changes occur because of myelination (adding new insulation) and pruning (getting rid of the extra connections we do not need).

Patience!

Now please be patient with me, and I promise I will get to the point.

The posterior (back) of the corpus callosum changes in size with age as the myelination and pruning activities of the brain change. On average, they increase with increased myelination and decrease with pruning.

Check out the following breakdown of how our brains change over time from birth to old age. The ages are approximate as every human's brain matures at a different rate dependent heavily upon genetics.

A Breakdown of Brain Maturity

Birth to 6 years—Humans are born with more neurons (wiring) than we will ever need to help us interpret the world we have just been born. The first three years of life are when we experience the most increase in brain activity as we learn to survive outside the womb.

Age 7-16 years—Our brains experience more significant growth in the anterior (front) region of the corpus callosum in a wave of development. This development could be because of a growing ability to use language and speech.

Age 17-20+ years— Although our brains have been cutting away unused and unneeded brain cells for many years, pruning of excess neurons (brain cells) begins in earnest and increases.

Age 20- 40+ years—a plateau of pruning and growth is reached. Our brains have reached a point where they are most fully developed. Brain maturity in most people is achieved here, and It is at this stage that connectiveness between neurons and the hemispheres of the brain become fully developed and rich.

During this stage is the point where I believe many who live with dissociative identity disorder begin to remember the severe trauma they experienced as children.

Let Me Ask You to be Patient with Me Just a Little Longer

I have stated in a previous post that the left hemisphere is responsible for interpreting the world about us, and the right for understanding what is being explained. The left hemisphere is the spokesman for the brain and right acts like its silent partner.

As I have said before, they have done experiments with people who have had their corpus callosum (wiring) cut between the two hemispheres of their brain to help end severe seizure activity. The results were stunning.

In one experiment they used headphones and told the person in their right ear (the right hemisphere because they have no communication to the left) to stand up, walk across the room and pick up a pencil. Immediately the person did as they were told. When the scientist asked this subject why he had done so, he reported feeling the need to walk, and he wanted a pencil.

The right brain heard the order and carried it out, but the left hemisphere had no idea that order had been given. To make sense of what the subject had just done, (i.e., standing up and going to get the pencil), the left hemisphere made up a scenario to explain what had just occurred.

The person who had just lied was unaware they had told a fib. To them, the answer they gave was the correct one without a doubt.

The Effects of Severe Childhood Trauma

Severe childhood trauma shuts down the left hemisphere (interpreter) and forces the brain to encode the memories of the event into the right (silent partner) hemisphere. As you may have surmised, if only the right hemisphere holds the memories, the person who experienced them cannot know about their existence, and they are "forgotten."

In this way life goes on, that is until the person reaches brain maturity when suddenly a new stage of development is reached, and the connections that had been lost due to the trauma are suddenly established. The result is a flood of memories from the trauma the person had experienced in childhood.

The Memories Aren't Lost

The memories aren't repressed, they aren't forgotten and then suddenly remembered. The new connections made between the two hemispheres of the brain have formed.

I think in children who have experienced horrendous and repeated trauma at an early stage in their brain development experience this effect to an even greater extent than do other adults.

The stress hormones that flood their little bodies and are never allowed to return to baseline cause an uptick in loss of connectedness between the two hemispheres of the brain.

The reason is that there is a significant dip in the formation of myelin (insulation) surrounding the fibres in their corpus callosum (wiring) at the point (age birth to 6 years) when our brains are just learning how to encode memories and how to survive outside the womb. It is easy to see how traumatic memories can be lost to the "waking self" as they are encoded on the right hemisphere, and the child simply moves on with life not even knowing those events had occurred.

Then when the child who had now developed dissociative identity disorder reaches adulthood (ages 20 – 40) and the connectiveness of the two hemispheres enters a new stage of development. Then these memories that have been filed away in the silent hemisphere of the brain suddenly burst into the consciousness of the left, and we are left scratching our heads and thinking we are crazy.

I know this is new information to many of us in the DID community, but I have included the links to the research I've been using to put this together. There is far more to the story to explore, but I wanted to bring you up to date on what I have found so far.

"We are our memories. That's all we are. That's what makes us the person we are. The sum of all our memories from the day we were born. If you took a person and replaced his set of memories with another set, he'd be a different person. He'd think, act, and feel things differently." Brian Falkner

References

At What Age Is the Brain Fully Developed? (2015). Mental Health Daily. Retrieved from:

https://mentalhealthdaily.com/2015/02/18/at-what-age-is-the-brain-fully-developed/

Blood Supply, Meninges, and Cerebrospinal Fluid Circulation. The Human Central

Nervous System (2008).

Springer, Berlin, Heidelberg https://doi.org/10.1007/978-3-540-34686-9_4

Luders, E., Thompson, Paul M., Toga Arthur W. (2010). The Development of the Corpus

Callosum in the Healthy Human Brain. Journal of Neuroscience, (30), 30-33

DOI:10.1523/JNEUROSCI.5122-09.2010

http://www.jneurosci.org/content/30/33/10985.short

McEwen, B. S., & Morrison, J. H. (2013). Brain On Stress: Vulnerability and Plasticity of the

Prefrontal Cortex Over the Life Course. NEURON, 79(1), 16–29.

http://doi.org/10.1016/j.neuron.2013.06.028

https://www.ncbi.nlm.nih.gov/pmc/articles/PMC3753223/

Ventricular System. Retrieved from:
https://en.wikipedia.org/wiki/Ventricular_system

The Freedom of Responsibility

Taking responsibility for one's own actions is a vital part of
healing from any disorder, but especially one as devastating as
dissociative identity disorder.

In this piece, we are going to examine the freedom that is gained
from doing so, and why it is so important.

The World of a Victim

Anyone who knows me understands that I feel strongly for
others who still live in the darkness of childhood trauma. I
suffered a long, long time from the events that occurred when I
was little that were entirely out of my control.

I lived in the world of victimization.

I felt strongly that every bad situation I found myself in as an
adult was directly related and caused by events that had occurred
when I was a kid.

Now, there can be absolutely no doubt but what the horrendous
things my abusers did to me were not my fault. Of course not.
Children are in no way responsible for the actions of an adult.
They cannot cause an adult to lust after them, nor can they stop
them from harming themselves.

The problem is that when you grow up a victim, it becomes who
you are in adulthood. I know I walked about bemoaning my then
present life feeling it was not happy because of what someone
else had done to me.

That is True, But...

To a certain extent, this was true. After all, no one will wake up every morning deciding to be miserable. No one would think, "I want to be lonely and afraid all the time."

Then one fateful day, I entered therapy.

My therapist, who is now retired, had a real mess on her hands. I was totally out of sync with what an adult was supposed to be, and I felt unable to change my life. She realized early on that I needed to be taught the very basics of life, including to take responsibility for my life.

Trauma-Time

The above doesn't sound too horrible at first glance. That is until you understand that I live with dissociative identity disorder and have more than 72 alternates. That doesn't mean I have 72 different people in my mind, that means that parts of my one personality were stuck in what is termed trauma-time.

Debra Wesselmann, MS, LIMHP, on her blog site gives the following definition of trauma-time:

"Trauma-time is a phenomenon that has grabbed and deceived almost every survivor of trauma at one point or another. Traumatic memories are stored differently than normal memories. They are encapsulated."

She states they are encapsulated, and that is the memories are set apart. As I have said in a previous article, the mechanism that causes this separation involves how the memories are encoded. However, that is not the focus of this piece.

The focus of this piece is the way since we have not only trapped these memories in events of the past but that we tend to relive those things and the emotions that go along them.

We Become Prisoners of Our Pasts

What I'm saying is that we become imprisoned in the past.

That may be an obvious statement to anyone who lives with dissociative identity disorder. We experience daily how our splintered minds can be triggered into reliving a horrible event from three decades before.

Upon being diagnosed with DID, inevitably we not only allow ourselves to be drawn into trauma-time with our alters, but we see our current lives through that lens also.

This lens I speak of is that all our problems are the fault of our former abusers.

I am in no way saying that the disorder and chaos of life as a multiple is our fault. Of course not. We did not cause our minds to splinter and we sure as hell didn't ask for the torture we underwent to become a dissociated mess.

However---

Here it comes folks, the hot water I mentioned in the first paragraph. Oh well, I've been in trouble before with people who have experienced trauma in childhood. We must keep up tradition.

Who Makes Our Decisions Today?

Are the problems we find ourselves experiencing the fault of those who hurt us so horribly in our pasts?

Things like getting into a bad marriage or getting pregnant at a young age. Things like not finishing college or working at a job we honestly hate.

Are these things entirely the fault of our pasts? Or are we responsible for the decision we make today?

I think you know my answer.

An Example from My Life

Yes, all humans are heavily influenced by the way they were brought up. Early family life gives us our window into society and how we should behave within it. However, once we reach adulthood, do we not make our own decisions?

I am in recovery from a prescription drug addiction. I was given pills for everything growing up, and I watched my mom pop pills and get high all my young life. Yes, her use of prescription drugs taught me that I can escape from reality if I got high.

Who was the lady who woke up in the dementia wing of a hospital when she had taken too many pills? Had someone held her mouth open and forced her to swallow them?

Wasn't it me?

The fault was mine. I had and still have the choice of following my upbringing or changing my life for the better.

The Magic Key

Being responsible for my own actions was a magic key that opened a door to a whole new avenue of thought. This road lead to more freedom that I ever thought existed.

You see, when I allowed myself to blame the trauma from my childhood on my decisions today, I gave up something wonderful!

The reality that I and only I am responsible for my decisions and actions.

What about the alters?

Another valuable lesson that my retired therapist had to teach me was that the alters, all of them, are me. I am them; they are me. Anything that is done in this body is my responsibility.

That meant I could no longer blame my actions when dissociated on an alter, and that meant I couldn't blame my past.

Ouch!

All the stupid, stupid decisions I have made as an adult are entirely and irrevocably my responsibility.

Period.

I Was Angry

I know those words hurt! They hurt me and made me extremely pissed off too!

That is until I began to understand the power that owning your behaviour and your decisions brings.

Not only this, but it brings freedom!

I am free to take pride in the right decisions I make and to feel frustrated at the bad ones.

I am open to saying, "Yes, I did that."

Not only this but I can say that without so without the hedge of blaming it on an alter.

They are me; I am them.

With This Freedom Comes Peace

With this power comes tremendous leaps forward into peace.
After I finally, after spending over seven years inpatient,
understood this principle I made tremendous strides.

Now I live with my alters well, and we have peace.

Oh, not the entire time. I still do and say things I do not
remember etc., but I am not worried because I know all the way
through that the buck stops here.

There is tremendous power in knowing and believing that no
one, and your past, cannot influence you. You are suddenly free
to be the person you were destined to be.

After all, isn't that what being in therapy is all about? Facing
who you are head-on and learning from what you see?

"Learning lessons is a little like reaching maturity. You're not
suddenly more happy, wealthy, or powerful, but you understand
the world around you better, and you're at peace with yourself.
Learning life's lessons is not about making your life perfect, but
about seeing life as it was meant to be." Elisabeth Kubler-Ross

Child Alters

I have a lot of lived experience with dealing with child alters.
My goodness, I have hundreds of six-year-old girls and boys and
at least one adorable three-year-old girl whose name is Mary
Ellen. I'll be using her as an example throughout this article.

Two Burning Questions

There are two burning questions people ask about child alters.
One is what are they? The other is Who are they?

I'll tackle the question of what they are first.

What are Child Alters

Child alters are you formed and trapped at different ages in
trauma-time (the actual time that a traumatic event occurred.)
For instance, Mary Ellen developed when I was around three
years and holds all the memories of traumatic events that
happened at that time in life.

No one understands yet just where in the brain alters are stored
(for lack of a better word.) What we do know is that a young
child's personality isn't fully formed and is pliable until they
reach around nine years of age.

Differences in Personality Formation

During these years children who are not experiencing severe and repeated traumatic events pull together all the parts of their personality (associate them.) They connect their memory directly linked to their experiences.

This connection is especially true of experiences and memories formed with their caregivers.

Children who are experiencing severe and repeated traumatic events are different. Their personalities miss the opportunity to pull together into a cohesive whole leaving the person splintered.

The experiences and memories of their caregivers remain dissociated.

No one understand how these disconnected (dissociated) clusters of memory and experience take on lives of their own and act independently of one another.

I think it has a lot to do with the formation of the amnesiac walls that are formed to protect the child. These occur so that they can carry on with life without going insane or killing themselves.

Memory is Not a Filing Cabinet

If you read my previous post on brain formation, you can see how this explainable.

The way memories are encoded and stored in the brain may be the answer.

In the brains of young children without trauma, memories are encoded and stored all over the brain.

It's not at all like the popular way people sometimes think of memory storage as a filing cabinet.

However, these "files" are connected so that if stimulated (triggered) one or more of them will bond together and you have a memory of what has happened in the past. This means you know how to handle what is occurred in the now because of memories of similar situations earlier in life.

In the brains of highly traumatized young children, the left hemisphere closes off, and the memories of the traumatic episode are encoded and stored in the right hemisphere **only**.

This storage problem is a massive problem because the right hemisphere is a silent and mute partner to the understanding and vocal left.

You can say that the left hemisphere doesn't know what the right hemisphere is doing.

Then Comes Brain Maturity

The memories that formed when I was 3 became encoded and silent. They were not lost, they were not repressed, they were merely put in an area that was entirely inaccessible to the child.

Consequently, they aren't retrievable to the adult survivor until brain maturity.

They Begin to Speak

At this point, because new connections made, the brain makes a huge leap. Some people suddenly remember, entirely unbidden, the things that happened in their childhood.

It is my belief, (this is not backed up yet by science), that all alters are memories stored in bundles. The memories are saved in the right hemisphere, and the amnesia experienced by many caused by the inability of the right and left hemispheres to speak before brain maturity.

That's the how, what about who?

Who are Child Alters?

Child alters are not strangers living in our heads. Neither are they demons, aliens, or monsters.

They are us, **all of them**.

Their experiences and emotions are ours, and all their behaviours are ours.

You cannot blame an alter for doing or saying something wrong because those actions are yours.

It's Normal to Fear Alters, but Then…

Mary Ellen is me when I was 3. She is adorable, and I'm very fond of her. That means I think of myself as being sweet and I am fond of me.

That's not wrong.

It's entirely okay to love myself.

When it can be hard, and I think every multiple reading this will agree, is when we don't like our alters or are afraid of them.

All of the above are involved in a very natural stage when first discovering their existence. However, that means you don't like and are afraid of ourselves.

When I first met Bianca, my precocious 18-year old self, I didn't like her at all.

I mean at all!

She was always buying things and has gotten me into trouble with the law at least twice.

However, after many years of working hard on these issues, I have discovered that Bianca is a beautiful ally!

Yes, she did illegal things from time to time, but her street smarts and determination to get things done is invaluable!

Bianca isn't someone else; she is me when I was 18. I am full of street smarts, and I am determined to get things done!

Bianca is me. I am Bianca.

It Isn't Easy

Reaching the point of acceptance of the different thoughts and memories of the alter is a milestone in recovery, but it isn't easy. Accepting that their memories, no matter how traumatic, are mine hurt like hell. Finally, I got it through my thick skull that their tears and hurts are mine.

How did I reach this point? By loving and accepting them. By becoming the mother to them (myself), I never had. I protect them, love them, cuddle them (in my mind of course), and will never, ever let anyone harm them again.

I have invited them to come live with me in the present, and they have accepted that invitation.

Common Misconceptions About Alters

As I have mentioned, alters are not demons to be cast out, or monsters in us set on destroying our lives. They are important. They kept us alive and prevented us from remembering horrible events so that we could carry on. It is essential to give credit where credit is due. They are the reason we are sane and alive today and deserve a lot of respect.

Integration

That having been said I'm going to speak now on integration. Integration is NOT where my personality or yours becomes wholly associated like people who haven't experienced severe and repeated childhood trauma.

That is impossible.

It is just as impossible for a "singleton" to become a "multiple."

Once past the age of association of the personality, the process of becoming a multiple cannot be reversed.

There have been experiments where a "singleton" was forced to form alters. However, these alters did not last. They broke down, and the person lost the ability to dissociate after a short time.

Integration is when the alters all agree on a leader and pull together to go in the same direction. It is when our actions and goals combine to form a formidable force for progress into the future.

It is like an orchestra, all playing their instruments extremely well, playing together in unison to make beautiful music. The leader who is chosen acts as the maestro, the person where the buck stops. The one who is out front, by agreement, to handle the outside world.

That is integration in a nutshell.

It takes a lot of practice, listening to each other, and helping each other to form this conglomeration. But it CAN be done; I am a living witness to this.

They Are Children

Child alters are not just an adult acting like a child, they ARE children. As such they are easily persuaded and harmed.

If Mary Ellen is "out" she (I) will only be 3. My actions,
thoughts, and behaviors will be those of a 3-year old child.

I'll tell a story on Mary Ellen (myself) that illustrates this and
the following point I want to make more clear.

A Story from My Own Life

Back in the early 90's when I first began treatment for DID, I
went to a picnic. Now the friends attending there knew me very
well and all about me living with DID. I trusted them implicitly.

I rode to the picnic with a lovely lady whose name was Gayle.
When we arrived at the house where the picnic was to be held,
and a tiny four-year little girl whose name was Elizabeth
greeting me when I opened the car door.

She said, "Hi, I'm Elizabeth. I'm four, want to play with me?"

Two hours later I "awoke" on the back deck of the house and
Gayle was approaching me with a newly grilled hamburger.

I looked at her and said "Gayle?"

She then told me that everything was okay, that I had just spent
the last two hours playing in the sandbox with Elizabeth. It was
then that I realized my clothes, including my bra, were full of
sand.

Elizabeth came up to me a few minutes later and was very
disappointed that her friend Mary Ellen was no longer able to
play.

It's Unlikely

One misconception a lot of people have is that child alter will
spontaneously appear.

Yes, like Mary Ellen and the sandbox episode, it can happen.
However, such events are tremendously rare. The reason is that

the child alters like any other children are not going to merely take over because they must feel comfortable and safe first.

This means that a child alter is unlikely to appear and take over in a busy place where they know no one.

I would never say it cannot happen. Every system is different. I am saying it can happen, there are always exceptions to the rule, but it is highly unlikely.

Please, Head tThe Following Warning

I have a warning I wish to convey. It is related to the sandbox episode.

Child alters, like other children, are very vulnerability!

They can easily be taken advantage of by strangers who wish to harm them. Had there been someone at that picnic who were sexual or otherwise predators, both Elizabeth and Mary Ellen would have been in danger.

Predators are NOT Just in Person. They Can Be Online

Please, please be very alarmed by people online in a chat room or a support group, or anywhere for that matter, who become extremely involved with your child alters.

Your inside children can be easily manipulated!

This means they are manipulating you!

Who I'm speaking of are people who talk to your child alters in private chat rooms or on any site telling them they love them or asking them to meet them somewhere. Just as you would if your inner child were an outside child, you should be terrified and keep them from making contact ever again.

Alert the administrator or owner of that site and do not allow anymore contact.

These trolls can be extremely dangerous and can bring harm to your system that can set back your recovery for years!

In Closing

I guess in closing I will say this. Child alters are beautiful and beautiful parts of you who never grew up. Like Peter Pan, they are still full of wonder and joy. Yes, they also remember some horrible things, but after those memories are dealt with you can enjoy the awe they still feel about the simple things in life.

Enjoy these little parts of you. They are precious.

"Life is full of beauty. Notice it. Notice the bumble bee, the small child, and the smiling faces. Smell the rain and feel the wind. Live your life to the fullest potential, and fight for your dreams." Ashley Smith

The Orchestra Analogy

There was once a large orchestra.

All the players in the orchestra were excellent at using their separate instruments, but they all played different music.

Each player insisted their music was what all should play, and they stubbornly went on day after day doing their own thing. Some even despised and hated the others even though they were in the same orchestra.

Some would play Beethoven, while others played Mozart.

The result was chaotic noise that pleased no one and got the orchestra nowhere. They all dreamed of becoming popular and playing music that caused their audiences to weep with pleasure, but they could not agree what or how to play.

Then one day a trained Maestro arrived and took up the baton. This person began working with the members of the orchestra, teaching them how to work together. He encouraged them to agree on and choose one song, the one that would make them famous.

Slowly, very slowly, the orchestra members began to understand that they must do as the Maestro suggested, or forever be lost in the chaos of the past.

The Maestro also made one more demand of the players. If they were going to play after he was retired and moved away, one of the orchestra members would have to assume the lead and take up the baton.

One of the strongest of the members agreed to do just that, and slowly, with agreement from the others, took over the work of the Maestro.

Then one miraculous day the orchestra, following the new Maestro's lead, began to play beautifully together.

They began playing before live audiences who gave standing ovations with tears streaming down their cheeks.

Together they had achieved their dream and thereafter were a success.

They had squabbles from time to time, and sometimes a member would decide to play their own tune during a performance. But most of the time the members relied on each other and worked together for the good of all.

This, to me, is what becoming co-conscious, cooperative, and integration is all about.

The members of the orchestra are the alters before treatment.

The first Maestro is a trained and caring therapist.

The second Maestro is the one alter that becomes the leader over the whole bunch.

The result of learning cooperation and co-consciousness (integration) is a successful future.

Explanation

This analogy illustrates what integrating is all about.

The members of the orchestra are the alters before treatment.
The first Maestro is their therapist.

It takes time, dedication and patience on the part of both the Maestro and the orchestra. But working together, a beautiful life forms out of the chaos.

Then one day, fusion happens. Will the orchestra never have problems? Of course not. However, after a while the person remembers the value of working together and chooses to work as one instead of many.

Body Image and DID

There are many parts of living with dissociative identity disorder that is difficult. They include not knowing from moment to moment if you have lost time, facing people who are upset because you have no idea what they are talking about and the never-ending fight to stay ahead of depression and anxiety. However, one of the most difficult and sometimes dangerous side-effects of living as a multiple is body image confusion.

I'm going to share with you my experience with this problem and speak about some solutions that may help.

Please Remember I'm Not a Therapist

However, I hope everyone remembers that not all multiple systems have the same problems. Every system is distinct having different aspects of the same issues. I am not a textbook case; there are none. There are as many ways to express multiplicity as there are people who live with it.

My Body Image

In my system, there are many different views on what the body looks. Some alters are six-years-old with very young agile bodies. Then there are some who are teens with raging hormonal bodies. Also, there are the alters who are in their 20s. Since there are tons of alters in my system, each of them has their own body image, including being male and female. The fact is that I (the waking-self) have my own body image which does not fit my 57-year old reality of a healthy 30-year old woman.

Problems with My Self-Image

The biggest problem for me is that these distorted images in body image that are all way off the mark. The reality is different in that my body is 57 going on 58, and has been through a major stroke, breast cancer and becoming a wheelchair user. My body is afflicted with several critical and potentially life-threatening conditions including diabetes type II, high blood pressure, and morbid obesity.

My body weighs 280 pounds, way too much for its 5'4" frame. Diabetes and many other disorders are the result of not owning the body, not feeding or caring for it correctly, and not paying attention when it cries out for help until I must.

Feeling like you are thirty when living in a body that is twice that age is a huge problem. Even after almost three decades of intensive psychotherapy, I feel disconnected with my body. My form is getting older and not doing very well. My legs are swollen, and I have begun to feel the pain of arthritis. My wheelchair limits my movements, but I often forget that I am not able to always do the things a walking person can do.

Sound Strange?

That may sound strange that I would forget I'm in a wheelchair, but it is true. That is how disconnected I am from what my body experiences. If I'm not careful, I will forget to feed or over feed my body. It's a constant battle to keep myself from getting hurt and a lot of frustration when I can't do things that I thought I should be able to do. I feel as though I do not live my body and that it is just an inconvenient thing that just hangs around and gets in my way.

It is easy to see how being so disconnected from one's body can be. If I don't acknowledge my body's age, size or condition my body will die, and I and my system die too.

The Treatment Takes Guts

How on earth can multiples get in contact with our bodies and treat them as parts of us instead of some strange hinderance?

The treatment for this problem is to use a mirror. I know that sounds horrendously scary as we have carefully built our self-images. If you are like me using a mirror makes you feel disgusted and terrified.

However, when I was challenged by my therapist to lay naked on my bed with a mirror and look at myself, I found after the shock has passed that I was not the ugly ogre I had been led to believe.

Why Do I Not Like What I See?

As a child, I heard multiple sources including the people who harmed me, my mother and other children that I was not beautiful. I was called fat, stupid, ugly and worthless. I internalized those messages, and that is why I abandoned my body. I have had the experiences of not being able to answer what colors are my eyes and hair when asked to renew my state identification card. There were several days two years ago that I looked at a mirror and didn't recognize the body that I was seeing. It was like seeing a stranger staring back at me.

Looking at oneself in the mirror is hard. Taking that glass thing and seeing all the imperfections and scars of the vessel that one lives in hurts. I know I heard the names they called me as a child and I saw the relics of what had happened to me during traumatic events.

Mirror therapy, I guess we'll call it, is enormously helpful, but excruciating.

Talk to Your Therapist First!

Please, talk to your therapist before you attempt mirror therapy. You'll need their support to work through the uncomfortable and sometimes dangerous emotions that seeing your body can bring to light. Those feelings were already there, looking at yourself as you are though, can be disturbing. Doing so is the first step towards living healthier.

Why I Bring This Up

I wanted to write this to let others out there who are living as I do, disconnected from their bodies, to see these words in black and white before them. Denial of this problem can be and is too often deadly. Obesity and the diseases I have mentioned are only the tips of the iceberg. There is anorexia, bulimia, and many other disorders that are the result of not caring for our bodies.

There is hope. I will keep working on this problem and hope one day to live in my body the way I was meant to from the beginning of my life.

"I know who I am. I am not perfect. I'm not the most beautiful woman in the world. But I'm one of them." Mary J. Blige

Trauma-Informed Care

Most of you, my readers, understand the definition of trauma having lived through more than enough as children. However, how many of you know what is meant by trauma-informed care?

In this article, we are going to explore what trauma-informed care is and the different ways it can be incorporated into a therapeutic relationship to help heal childhood trauma.

What Is Trauma-Informed Care?

To be honest, I've heard the term trauma-informed care, but until I researched for this article, I had no idea what that meant. So, I did a thorough search to find out the answer to the question what "is trauma-informed care?" So, bear with me as I tackle this subject.

Trauma-informed care is a structured treatment that involves understanding, recognizing and responding to the effects of all sorts of trauma. The therapist helps a traumatized client by creating a sense of physical, psychological and emotional safety for their client and themselves.

SAMHSA (Substance Abuse and Mental Health Services Administration) has spent a lot of time and money outlining how it sees trauma-informed care.

In one downloadable PDF, I found some beneficial information describing what trauma-informed care is all about. SAMHSA emphasizes the three E's, events, the experience of events and effects of traumatic events.

Let me break that down for you.

Events. A traumatic event can occur anytime during a lifetime and include a sense of extreme threat of physical or psychological harm or severe and life-threatening neglect. A traumatic event may happen once in a person's lifetime or be repeatedly perpetrated against a child or an adult.

SAMHSA gives the above description of a traumatic event that falls in line with what the Diagnostic and Statistical Manual of Mental Disorders Edition 5 (DSM-5) states.

Experience of Events. The way people experience a traumatic event is different for each individual. What is traumatic for one, may not be for another. A lot depends on how we interpret our physical and psychological well-being both during and after trauma.

One example is child sexual abuse perpetrated against a very young child where the child does not experience fear. Yes, it is very wrong and is later harmful to them as an adult, but if the child does not know that what they are experiencing is not supposed to happen, in the absence of fear they have no reason to interpret it as traumatic.

It is later, when the child becomes an adolescent or an adult, that the shame and guilt of what has been done to them arises. So, although they were not traumatized while children, a discovery that what was done to their bodies is the trigger for the trauma.

It is also essential to remember that although we may think of trauma as happening in childhood, trauma occurs to adults as well. Tornadoes, hurricanes, volcanic eruptions, car accidents, the sudden death of a child, all are horrendously traumatizing. Let's not forget about the war. Many war veterans suffer horribly from the traumatic events and sights they were forced to endure in the service to their country.

Effects of Traumatic Events. Trauma has lots of long-lasting after effects, some of them life-altering. Although we are familiar with trauma creating chaos in someone's life immediately after the event, sometimes the consequences can be delayed for decades.

Sometimes we are unable to connect the traumatic event or events to what we are seeing in our own behavior.

I experienced the childhood trauma I lived through as a series of events I conveniently forgot. I would just push it over there so that I could exist and carry on over here. Thus, I formed alternative egos to hold the memories with all the terror and pain. I didn't begin to be traumatized until the memories of those events began to return almost three decades later spontaneously.

I experienced flashbacks, nightmares, losing time, and depression so deep that I was hospitalized more than thirty times, one of them lasting for over seven and a half years.

Other more typical examples of someone responding to trauma are having problems with relationships, managing thinking processes like memory, attention, and thinking and regulating the expression of emotion.

The Physical Changes from Trauma

Trauma that is experienced in childhood changes structures in our brain. Through fMRI imaging and other techniques researchers have found that adults who suffered trauma in childhood have measurably smaller hippocampi and amygdalae than average adults. In some people, such as those who have post-traumatic stress disorder or a dissociative disorder like DID, the differences are remarkable.

One scientific paper found on the US National Library of Medicine National Institute of Health website reported on just such a study. In it the researchers found DID patients to have 19.2% smaller hippocampal and 31.6% smaller volumes compared to healthy subjects.

The hippocampus is responsible for memory consolidation and retrieval. So, it is not unreasonable to think that because ours is not the correct size, the memory lapses we have during a split are connected to this size difference.

The amygdala is vital to our ability to interpret and respond to danger. Even if we do not at first succeed in identifying something as dangerous, this part of our brain is quick to respond. When a threat is detected, the amygdala sends out emergency signals to the rest of the body getting it ready to flee, fight, or freeze. It takes no leap of the imagination to see the correlation between a damaged amygdala and hypervigilance, flashbacks, and fugue.

The Guidelines for Trauma-Informed Care

 According to SAMHSA, trauma-informed care helps adults understand that their behaviors are coping strategies designed to overcome and survive adversities they have faced in life. Since the traumatic events are overwhelming and the survivor had no power to help themselves, they are acting out trying to protect themselves from a danger that no longer exists.

Remember, trauma doesn't necessarily mean experiencing someone mistreating or threatening you. It can also take the form of hearing the traumatic events of another person being retold as they relive it. Thus, therapists are very much in the firing line of becoming traumatized themselves.

When treating children, trauma-informed care providers must utilize other healthcare and protective agencies to not only protect their small clients but to safeguard their own mental health.

The first step in treating someone who has been traumatized is recognizing that it has occurred. This can be more difficult and tricky than it sounds. Depending on their gender, age, and other demographic information, the person may be very protective of the information that they were the victim of trauma.

Sometimes people are forced into therapy by law enforcement, the court or by a partner who is threatening to leave. In these cases, the survivors may not understand themselves that they are a victim.

Men especially find it hard to disclose any type of abuse or trauma they are or have gone through. Men can be and are victims of violence in the home too and must not be forgotten in the trauma formula.

It can be tricky for providers to give their client a label of trauma survivor for one big reason.   A therapist cannot ask about or imply that someone has a trauma history. To do so would jeopardize the treatment because they could accidentally implant the idea of trauma where none may not exist. They must wait to see what the client discovers on their own and be there to help them accept and later recover from it.

The 6 Principles of a Trauma-Informed Care Approach

SAMHSA outlines six critical principles for therapists to follow when offering treatment, trustworthiness, peer support, collaboration, empowerment and cultural/gender issues.

Safety. No matter the age of the person being treated, it is essential that the client feel physically and psychologically safe. This gives the client the ability to open up to their therapist and explore what happened, how it affected them, and how to heal.

Trustworthiness. This isn't necessarily meant for the client, but rather to the therapist who needs to remain open and honest with their clients. Its only with this honesty that people like myself who have been so hurt by those who should have treated me well can learn to trust anyone, especially a therapist.

Peer Support. It is no secret that SAMHSA is a big fan of peer support. When people are in pain, they naturally want to turn to others who understand where they have been and what they are going through. A peer is someone with lived experience of trauma. Also known as survivors, we help each other by sharing what has worked for us and hold each other up when times get tough.

I found tremendous peer support through Ivory Garden DID Support Group. Found at IGDID.com, Ivory Garden helped me come to terms with my own DID, and I made some lifelong friends along the way. When I was diagnosed with breast cancer and faced having my right breast removed, my friends at Ivory Garden were there supporting me. Granted it is online peer support, but it was beautiful anyway.

Collaboration. This term is centered on the staff of the clinic or hospital that offers trauma-informed care. SAMHSA believes that good cooperation among all the staff of a center offering trauma support is crucial to modeling the sharing of power and equality of relationships to the clients.

They quote one expert as stating, "One does not have to be a therapist to be therapeutic."

Empowerment. By recognizing that all people have strengths and abilities, the trauma-informed approach stresses these to try and build resiliency in their clients. The therapist recognizes that his/her clients have come to them for help and they endeavor to give assistance and support.

Cultural and Gender Issues. A trauma-informed therapist tries to move past cultural stereotypes and biases against any client for their race, ethnicity, sexual orientation, age, religion or gender identity. This type of therapist will incorporate processes that are responsive to the needs of their clients based on their needs and address historical traumas that they may have experienced.

I Know, a Little Dry Wasn't It?

I realize that this topic is a little dry to chew on but understanding what trauma-informed care is more critical now than ever before. Therapists are more and more turning to this type of therapy model to help their clients, so it behooves us to try to understand the process and goals of it as much as possible.

As a trauma survivor, I hope that the understanding of what trauma does and how to prevent it in the first place becomes paramount in our world. If we can keep children from experiencing adverse experiences such as any type of abuse and help adults who have become victims, then we will have come very far indeed in stamping out unnecessary suffering.

Child abuse is preventable and so is domestic violence of any kind. That means that there need not be a massive world population of traumatized adults trying their best to survive.

"A controlled child also learns that the default human approach to interaction is forcing, threatening, or manipulating others. Alternatively, they may come to believe that they are 'destined' to be a giver who never receives anything back."
~Darius Cikanavicius,

Change the Language to Change the Conversation

The words we use to describe ourselves have a huge impact on how we are treated. If we call ourselves by a term that means something negative, we will inevitably be treated in a negative fashion.

There are terms used to describe those of us who live with mental health conditions. However, those words, including the ones I just used, must be changed. This is the only way to get people looking at diagnoses such as bipolar disorder and schizophrenia differently and opening an open and honest dialogue within the community.

Some will say I'm being politically correct in what I'm about to share with you, but that's not true. Words carry meaning and no matter how you are politically aligned or even if you are not, we all understand how a word or phrase can make us feel. We all know how labels can determine our fundamental thoughts about ourselves and how we are seen by the community.

We must change our language if we wish to move forward.

I'm going to talk about each of the terms I am speaking of in the following paragraphs, as well as offer suggestions on how to change the language.

Stigma.

The word stigma has no immediate meaning to many in the community.

The Merriam-Webster Dictionary defines the word stigma like this:

A Definition of stigma

1 a. archaic: a scar left by a hot iron b: a mark of shame or
discredit c: an identifying mark or characteristic; 2 a: a small
spot, scar, or opening on a plant or animal b: the usually apical
part of the pistil of a flower which receives the pollen grains and
on which they germinate.

https://www.merriam-webster.com/dictionary/stigma

As can be seen, even looking up the word in a dictionary does
little to explain what stigma is about.

I'll give you a one-word definition that we should use instead.

Discrimination.

Discrimination is a word that everyone can understand. It is
exactly what is happening to people with a brain disorder when
we are our medical insurance doesn't cover all our needs but
does any other medical issue. This word carries weight because
this is something our society has been grappling with for
decades.

 Persons with brain disorders do not have adequate housing, are
forced to live in the streets, and are treated like they do not
belong in society. We are ostracized from churches, made fun of
in school, and feared. If that is not discrimination, then I do not
know what is.

 People in the United States march in the streets to end
discrimination against people of color, and the LGBTQ
community. Yet we sit quietly by while people who need
specialized care for brain disorders suffer in silence.

I believe that by changing the word from stigma, which does not
fit, to brain disorder, which does we can change this tragic
misjustice.

Mental Illness

This is the term that is the most defining. I am not ill. I live a very healthy and happy life under a doctor's care, just like someone with diabetes or thyroid dysfunction.

I live with a brain disorder, as do all people who are living with a diagnosis that requires a Psychiatrist, a specialized medical doctor. Can you see how saying to someone you know, "I have a brain disorder" sounds less frightening and more accurate?

Allow me to offer two scenarios to show you what I mean.

Scenario One.

Your son has just been diagnosed in the hospital with schizophrenia, and your neighbor visits you to see how things are going. She asks you what is wrong with your son, and you tell her your son was just diagnosed with a serious mental illness. Your neighbor leaves and tells your other neighbors in whispers and hushed tones about your son. After this you rarely hear from any of your other neighbors again.

Motivated by fear, they silently peek out their curtains at you as you get in your car to go and visit him fearful of what he might be like and do when he gets home.

Scenario Two.

Your son has just been diagnosed with schizophrenia, and your neighbor visits you to see how things are going. She asks what is wrong, and you tell her your son was just diagnosed with a serious brain disorder. Your neighbor leaves and goes to your other neighbors and they organize a food service for you. They keep doing so for a week while you are traveling back and forth to the hospital visiting your son. Motivated by empathy, your neighbors shower you with warm casseroles and get-well cards and look up the disorder you told them about on their computers to see what they can do to help.

The above scenarios aren't far-fetched. I wish they were. Changing a term makes all the difference in the world about how you are seen and how other people respond to you. How many families have received the devastating news that their son or daughter has a severe brain disorder only to find themselves set adrift in the sea of loneliness because the people around the see them through eyes full of fear. This terror is so bad that most people will write off this family, reassuring themselves that it will never happen to them.

Even faith communities tell themselves that this family is in pain not because their child's brain is malfunctioning but from punishment. They may feel their child's "craziness" must have been something evil in either the parents or the child that warranted their suffering.

Changing the thinking of those around us can help to end these tragedies.

Consumer

This term is by far the one I find most derogatory.

People unfamiliar with being a client hear this word and immediately in conjures up in their minds thoughts of resources being used up. Nothing could be farther from the truth. People with brain disorders are not using up anything. Yes, the procedures, medications and help we need to battle our chronic brain disorders are expensive, but that's because of the discriminatory pricing of the things we need.

Check out the price differences between the services required by a person with a brain disorder as compared to someone with diabetes type one.

The prices compared.

- The cost of seeing a Psychiatrist (Brain Disorder Specialist) is $350/session
- The cost of seeing an Endocrinologist (Diabetes Specialist) is $100/visit
- The cost of seeing a Therapist is $250/session
- The cost of seeing a General Practitioner is $80/visit
- The cost of Latuda $1,258/month
- The cost of Insulin $100-$200/month

It should be evident from the prices above that treating brain disorders costs much more than treating even common disorders such as diabetes.

Faulty Thinking

There is also the faulty thinking that states, "Why should I pay for people who are chronically ill, I'm not." Also, people are prone to believing this is, "someone else's problem, not mine. It will never happen to me."

No one can say definitively they and their family are immune to any chronic disease.

In our society diabetes and obesity are rampant. To be frank, with the growing uncertainty, unrest and loneliness growing in our communities and homes, no one is immune from becoming despairing and suffering from a brain dysfunction themselves.

If you are thinking there are more people with diabetes than a brain disorder, think again. According to the National Institute of Mental Health (NIMH), One in five (20%) of the population of the United States are diagnosed with a brain disorder.

Now contrast that figure with this figure from the U.S. Center for Disease Control (CDC) which reports that approximately one in nine (9.3%) people in the United States are live with a diabetes. So, the thinking process that states that brain disorders are not as important to treat as diabetes fly out the window.

These statistics prove that your family is more likely to have a member diagnosed with a brain disorder and require lifelong medications and treatment than to develop diabetes.

No one is immune. No one.

When the tragedy of a chronic medical condition visits you or your family, and statistically speaking, it will, who will pay for your care?

Simply Change the language

I realize the state of Illinois has been pressuring to change discriminatory labelling to "person first language", but more must be done and now is the time.

This discussion has involved only a few of the words and phrases that must be changed in our daily conversations. Opening a nationwide discussion on brain disorders and language must happen if we are to gain ground in our fight.

Ending the discrimination against those of us who live daily with severe brain disorders is paramount. There is no other way that I see, that will get our word out more powerfully than to simply change the language.

"I hated labels anyway. People didn't fit in slots--prostitute, housewife, saint--like sorting the mail. We were so mutable, fluid with fear and desire, ideals and angles, changeable as water." Janet Fitch

Somatic Symptoms and Dissociative Identity Disorder

Some who read my blog may find this post upsetting and I understand. I'm going to be walking on holy ground for many of us who live with dissociative identity disorder.

I have lived dissociative identity disorder all my life, but now a new diagnosis has been added to explain my physical discomfort. Somatic symptom disorder (SSD) formerly known as somatization disorder).

The latter disorder is the one this article is about.

I want to ask one huge favor of all my readers. I'm going to be speaking on a very touchy subject for some of us. Talking about the pain that we feel but that has no basis in physical facts is a holy-shit topic for many. I know, I have felt this way many times.

Let me make it perfectly clear that I am absolutely not saying here that any of you or I are faking. Nope. I'm not. Just read the article through before you judge me too harshly. I'm writing from experience as one of you, not some doctor trying to say you are a nut case.

So, hang onto your hats everyone, the ride might get pretty bumpy.

My Recent Health Scare

As many of my readers know, I've been having some physical problems lately. I have had massive headaches, dizziness, blurry vision and a lot of other neurological symptoms. I grew frightened because I had triple negative breast cancer in 2014 and had my right breast completely removed.

I went to my doctor. She brushed me off saying I needed physical therapy. I felt frustrated with her for not listening to me and changed doctors.

This doctor listened and decided to be safe we would do an MRI with contrast to have a look.

I saw him again on Friday to get the results.

My brain looks fairly normal. They did find signs of the small strokes (transient ischemic attacks) I've had. They also found a few regions in my brain were undersized.

Since I have DID, that wasn't surprising to me at all.

What they didn't find was any reason for my symptoms. I was very frustrated and upset because I have been and still do feel like shit.

"What is going on?" I begged him.

His answer, "Would you like to increase your antidepressant?"

What I Heard Verses What He Said

To say I was dismayed plays down the strong emotions that flooded me. Like all of you, I spent my entire childhood having people refusing to listen to me. Even when I was seven, the doctors didn't listen to me after I tried to leap from a ledge more than thirty floors above a busy Memphis highway.

During the fifteen years, I was being brutally abused, I tried in many ways to get help without saying the words, but my teachers, doctors, Sunday school teachers, and other adults wouldn't listen.

When I grew into a young adult, I had all kinds of nasty
neurological symptoms. Basically, they were very much the
same as those I've been having lately. There again I went to
doctors to find out what the hell was wrong with me. I was
ignored for the most part, until I went to a neurological clinic in
St. Louis, Missouri.

The doctor who saw me in the St. Louis Neurological Clinic told
me I needed desperately to lose weight, lower my stress level
and get off the midnight shift I had been working for almost
three years.

When Reality Bites You in the Ass

I felt insulted. There WAS something wrong with me, I just
knew it. However, I took his advice. I got off the midnight shift
for evenings, lost a lot of weight and moved out on my own
away from my family of origin who was dedicated to living a
life in crisis.

Does this scenario sound familiar from the first few paragraphs?

After I had forced myself to calm down inside, I thought about
what my new doctor had said and pondered.

The symptoms I have been having in the past year that have
been getting gradually worse almost exactly mirror those I had
in the 1980s.

It's from this point on that this article can set people off. I want
you all to remember, I AM NOT talking about you, I AM talking
about ME.

The greatest reason I have been feeling so badly this past year is
that I do not take care of myself. My body is rebelling from a
form of self-induced abuse.

I have gained 50 pounds in this past year, I eat too much
artificial sweetener and I do not exercise at all. I sit in my
recliner and do nothing but exercise my fingers when I type.
That's it.

If you think that you can't eat too much sweetener, think again. I used Aspartame for years until I began to have some serious mental health issues unrelated to the DID diagnosis. Now I've been using generic Splenda and am beginning to have some of the same things happening.

You see, I don't just put one or two sweeteners in a cup of coffee, I must have more than four or I'm not satisfied. That means, on an average day I might consume more than twenty of the packets!

Way, way too much!

Setting Priorities and Getting My Act Together

Losing weight is a priority. I now weight almost 300 lbs. again, something I swore I would never do again.

While I was listening to the doctor Friday, he told me about a phone app that would help me keep track of my calories and other nutrients. Instead of feeling defensive and angry like I have I times past, I really listened and decided to take him up on his idea.

Not only am I now keeping close track of what goes down my gullet, but I'm also cutting way back on sweetener. I will not completely stop using it because I cannot consume sugar, however, I will no longer use more than ten a day. If I still don't feel right, I'll cut it back more.

I am not going to starve myself, that is counterproductive. I'm going to feed my body nutritious food and keep calories for later in the day when I usually watch YouTube and want to snack.

It's time I stop living to eat and begin eating to live.

In other words, I'm getting my act together.

My Questions I Asked Myself and the Answers I Came to Understand

As I have examined my "illness", I realized there was more going on here than met the eye. It wasn't just my diet and lack of exercise that was making me have the symptoms that have both frightened me and slowed me down. There is another problem lurking in the dark that is harming me, somatic symptom disorder.

When the doctor first announced to me that they could find nothing wrong, I wanted to weep. I would have had I not been in the presence of a stranger. I found myself asking familiar questions in my mind.

With the help of my therapist later that same morning after my doctor's appointment, I have settled for the following answers to those questions.

Am I just looking for attention?

No, my therapist assured me. Why would I look for attention by "pretending" to be sick? I have taken control of my life as much as anyone can with dissociative identity disorder and I am very involved with advocacy. I have no reason to look for attention from doctors when I have a growing career.

Are my symptoms in my mind?

Yes, and no.

Somatic Symptom Disorder (SSD)

While discussing my problem with my therapist that morning, I was reminded of something I had read about but paid little attention to. Perhaps I should have looked at it better because it turns out I not totally responsible for my symptoms as they are directly related to my childhood.

I am living with a coexisting condition known as somatic symptom disorder (SSD). A simple explanation of what constitutes this disorder is as follows:

Somatic symptom disorder is a form of mental illness that causes one or more bodily symptoms, including pain. The symptoms can involve one or more different organs and body systems, such as:

- Gastrointestinal symptoms: abdominal pain, nausea

- Pain: joint pain, pain in the extremities

- Cardiopulmonary symptoms: shortness of breath, chest pain, dizziness

- Conversion symptoms: difficulty swallowing and walking

- Neurological Symptoms: migraines, blurry vision

- Reproductive Symptoms: irregular and painful menstruation

Before we go on, it is vital to remind everyone that these aches, pains and other symptoms are not fake. They are very real and are disruptive to life.

In a paper published in 1994 by Glenn N. Saxe and company in the American Journal of Psychiatry reported a study to see the correlation between people living with DID (then called multiple personality disorder) and what was then called somatization disorder.

They concluded the following after studying people who live with DID against those who do not.

"Somatization disorder (somatic symptom disorder) is a frequent and serious comorbid disorder among patients with dissociative disorders."

In fact, in their study, 80% of the patients with dissociative disorders reported headaches, a finding that was consistent with other studies examining the same or similar issues.

What Causes Somatic Symptom Disorder

There is a lot of speculation for the causes of somatic symptom disorder. However, in a paper I found published by the American Journal of Psychiatry by Dr. Richard J. Brown and associates in 2005 can help shed some light.

They found that somatization disorder (now called somatic symptom disorder) was heavily present in patients who reported severe emotional and physical abuse. They also found that sexual abuse, separation/loss and witnessing violence, anything their subjects went through as children that conflicted with their need for a cohesive family were huge factors in forming SDD.

To quote the paper, "Somatization disorder patients reported significantly greater childhood emotional abuse and more severe forms of physical abuse, relative to the comparison subjects, with chronic emotional abuse being the best predictor of unexplained symptoms."

It is totally no surprise that adults who experienced violations against their bodies and minds as children would grow up to have difficulty understanding the sensations we feel and misread the signals.

We swing from one extreme to another. We worry too much about that ache we have in the back of our head, or we totally ignore it. Either way, such a misunderstanding of our bodies wreaks havoc on our lives.

What Shall We Do to Heal?

Somatic symptom disorder, as I have said, is not a case of malingering or pretending to have pain. The pain is real and needs to be addressed by your healthcare practitioner. They must rule out, as did my MRI, that there is nothing physically wrong causing your discomfort.

That is number one.

Then, if the tests come back normal, it's time to listen without judgment to what your provider has to say. They may not understand fully what they are seeing, but a good Therapist or Psychiatrist would.

The first thing you be thinking is, "Isn't there a quick fix, like a magic pill that will fix me?"

Let me state this for the record:

There are no magic pills.

There never was nor is there likely to be in the future.

However, antidepressant medications are often prescribed, but they only address the underlying emotional issues and even they take a while to help.

I looked on the Mayo Clinic website to see what they recommended. Although these ideas are not specifically for people who live with DID or other effects from childhood trauma, they make pretty good sense.

The first thing they state is that the goal of treatment is to improve your symptoms and your ability to function.

The next recommendation the Mayo Clinic site gives is to seek out psychotherapy. I know, I know, many of us are already in psychotherapy for our childhood trauma issues, so mentioning this may seem redundant. However, you and I both know how horribly stressful working on these issues is for us. The anxiety, depression, and just plain fear that accompany working on the issues we must face are daunting.

- The type of psychotherapy mentioned on the Mayo Clinic site is cognitive behavioral therapy (CBT).

The reasons CBT can help are:

- It will help you examine and adapt your beliefs about the physical sensations in your body

- Help you learn ways to reduce stress

- Help you learn to cope when physical symptoms occur

- Help reduce your preoccupation with your symptoms

- Help eliminate your avoidance of situations and activities because they are uncomfortable

- Aid in addressing the mental health disorder that you have developed due to your childhood adverse experiences

How Does It Help Me to Recognize My Somatic Disorder?

Now that I know that, other than being in a wheelchair and being very obese, I am basically very healthy. Now I can concentrate on losing the weight and being more active.

However, for me, it is more than that.

I am beginning to concentrate more on where I can go from here. I have gotten the spunk back I had lost and am ready to push forward once more.

Just like with the other issues surrounding the childhood trauma I endured as a kid, I'm ready to conquer this issue too. It will not win. I will succeed.

I am not imagining the aches and pains I feel. They are real. However, now I understand I do not need to panic because I am okay. I know the steps I need to make myself feel better and can move on.

I saw the following quote and loved it. It seems so apt to put at the end of this article.

"Far better is it to dare mighty things, to win glorious triumphs, even though checkered by failure than to rank with those poor spirits who neither enjoy much nor suffer much, because they live in a gray twilight that knows not victory nor defeat." Theodore Roosevelt

It is the suffering we have endured that makes multiples special, not the disorder itself. Please, try to remember that.

Insights on Suicide from Someone Who Has Survived

Choosing to die by suicide has become an epidemic in the United States. I lost my mother to it in 2012 and have almost become a statistic at least three times.

As many of you know already, I recently gave a short speech at a function to raise awareness of choosing to die by suicide. All the performers that evening either were suicide survivors themselves or family members of someone who died.

One young lady broke my heart as she sang about the death of her sister and her tears filled my heart with grief.

I was there that evening to speak to those who, like this hurting young lady, to those who were survived an attempt, and for those who might have been there that night thinking of dying at their own hand.

The Tragedy of Suicide by the Numbers

I hate to sit here and quote stats at you, but I think they help bring a sense of reality to what I'm talking about.

Every day, approximately 123 Americans die by suicide. (CDC)

There is one death by suicide in the US every 12 minutes. (CDC)

Suicide takes the lives of over 44,965 Americans every year. (CDC)

The highest suicide rates in the US are among Whites, American Indians and Alaska Natives.

An estimated quarter million people each year become suicide survivors (AAS).

There is one suicide for every estimated 25 suicide attempts. (CDC)

There is one suicide for every estimated 4 suicide attempts in the elderly. (CDC)

1 in 100,000 children ages 10 to 14 die by suicide each year. (NIMH)

7 in 100,000 youth ages 15 to 19 die by suicide each year. (NIMH)

12.7 in 100,000 young adults ages 20-24 die by suicide each year. (NIMH)

Suicide is the 3rd leading cause of death for 15 to 24-year old Americans. (CDC)

Suicide is the 4th leading cause of death for adults ages 18-65. (CDC)

Lesbian, gay, and bisexual young people who come from families that reject or do not accept them are over 8x more likely to attempt suicide than those whose families accept them.

Each time an LGBTQ person is a victim of physical or verbal harassment or abuse, they become 2.5x more likely to hurt themselves.

Source of Information

A Voice from a Very Dark Place

As I sat and listened to the music being performed and the people around me speak, I grew aware that many were in an extremely dark place. I overheard one woman tell another about her son who had died and another about her sister.

So, when it came my time to perform, I felt I had arrived at a special place. I had the opportunity to share with those in the audience what it was like to decide to die.

I began by reading an edited version of my post, The Danger of the Wave I had written in June of 2018. In my post, I had explained the wave of relief I had felt after I took an overdose in 1995 which I almost did not survive. That evening when I almost died, I suddenly found I wasn't afraid or anxious anymore, I was at peace with the knowledge that I would never have to wake up again.

Then I went to bed to die.

I then spoke about the reasons people die by suicide. It isn't to harm someone else or get back at them, and it isn't out of anger at someone else, it is because of the horrendous emotional pain I was in.

Afterwards, I moved on to words of hope I had learned from that very dark place.

I told the family members who had lost their beloveds that they were not responsible for the actions their loved one took. As family, they were not capable of stopping someone who truly wanted to die.

I told the people who had survived like I did that I understood what they were going through. Even after twenty-three years, there are still people who say unkind words about my attempt. They feel bitter and afraid.

Words of Hope from Someone Who Understands

After I spoke to the audience about the other aspects of death by suicide, it was time to speak to anyone who was there who may be thinking about dying.

These are the same words I wish to offer to all of you this evening.

There is no one in the entire universe like you.

That makes you unique, one-of-a-kind, and special.

If you die, humanity will lose a piece of ourselves.

You are the only voice who can help someone else who is struggling.

Your voice may be the one who changes the destiny of all mankind.

Ordinary People Can Change the World

To those who sniff at the above words, let me remind you that history is replete with interventions by ordinary people that have changed the direction of the world.

The two people I'm going to write about below are famous today, but they both had humble beginnings. Had they chosen to die, the world as we know it could not exist.

Rosa Parks. Mrs. Rosa Parks was born and raised in Alabama to a couple who were former slaves. The family lived on a farm where she once stood in front of the house with her family and watched while the Ku Klux Klan marched down the road.

After marrying Raymond Parks, in 1943 she became involved in the civil rights movement.

Rosa Parks was an ordinary person with a high school education who one day made a decision that made history.

On December 1, 1995 Rosa Parks was on her way home on a bus from a long day at work. She had taken a seat in the first rows of seats designated for "colored" passengers. At that time, the law required that African-Americans sit in the back of the bus while Caucasian-Americans sat in the front.

As the bus Mrs. Parks rode on continued to run its route, the "white section" filled up and the bus driver noticed that white passengers were needing to stand in the aisle. He stopped the bus and moved the sign that separated the two sections back one row leaving the seat in which Mrs. Parks sat in the "white only" section.

The law at that time gave bus driver's the right to call the Montgomery, Alabama police should a black passenger refuse to move.

Rosa Parks knew this, yet when the bus driver insisted that she give up her seat to allow white people to use it, Mrs. Parks did a brave thing, she stood her ground.

The driver demanded, "Why don't you stand up?" to which Rosa replied, "I don't think I should have to stand up."

The driver called the police and had her arrested.

The brave act of one small Alabaman seamstress changed the course of the history of the United States forever.

Albert Einstein. Although Albert Einstein is considered one of the world's great geniuses today, it wasn't always so.

Einstein was born in 1881 and was very slow in learning to speak. Even after he did start talking, he often whispered to himself before saying the words out loud.

The family decided to give him the nickname "the dopey one."

When Einstein turned 21, he graduated from Zurich Polytechnic, Switzerland in 1900. His grades were good but not stellar, in fact his marks were the lowest in his math courses!

After he graduated with his diploma as a Physics and Mathematics teacher, Einstein was unable to find work.

The problem? Einstein's professors had labeled him a troublemaker and a disobedient student, then refused to give him the necessary good references to teach.

Because of his inability to find work, Einstein's father wrote to friends asking if they would hire his son, but his attempts failed.

Einstein's father later declared on his death bed to Einstein that his son was a great disappointment to him.

Finally, in 1903, a friend of Albert Einstein's found him a job at a patent office as a patent investigator. There he would spend a few hours evaluating the submitted patents he had been given to investigate and then used the rest of his time doing thought experiments and reading scientific papers.

Two years later, this unknown "dopey", troublemaker, patent office clerk wrote the scientific paper, "The Special Theory of Relativity." His paper would turn the world of physics on its head and change the world forever.

How Does Any of This Pertain to You?

Had either Rosa Parks or Albert Einstein died before their time, our world would be completely unrecognizable today.

The reason is simple and elegant.

None of us lives in a vacuum, we are all intricately connected beyond any disconnection.

For an example I site myself.

Had I died in February 1995, the DID community would be minus one very loud advocate for the truth about the disorder.

I would never have written this blog and there are lives who may have been unreachable by anyone else's voice.

I know for a fact that at least one life was saved when I gave the speech "The Danger of the Wave" last week. A person who was there told me someone had received a healthy dose of hope.

I am humbled.

I guarantee, you probably do not understand just how valuable you are and how losing your light prematurely would be a great tragedy to the whole world.

Choosing to Live

Let's get one thing very clear.

I'm not saying you are not in pain and that you should live on for someone else.

No.

Not at all.

What I am saying is that choosing to live and face your fears and pain is more than something someone else wants you to do, it is downright heroic.

We do decide to live can take the horrible pain and suffering we feel and turn it into something beautiful.

Its people like you and I who are so passionate who can use our energy to propel the world forward and bring peace, one person at a time.

I want to force you to listen, but I know I can't.

Only you can do that.

It's up to you to find the courage to go on, even when you don't want to.

I've had many opportunities to end my existence since 1995 and believe me sometimes I feel it would be better.

However, my natural curiosity has kept me going.

I want to see what's around the next corner, what good things I would miss should I die?

I just wanted to impart to you a little of that curiosity and hope today.

Choose to live because you want to know how you can help others, or simply because what goes down must go up.

If your life is in the toilet tonight, well, tomorrow or next week things must only go up from here.

Please, choose to live.

I'll leave you with a quote from Henna Sohail:

"And one day, as she was buried deep in her thoughts,
she heard a still small voice ask her,

'If you could go back in life,
what would you have done differently?'

And without missing a beat
she answered, 'I would have chosen me'

And finally, she made the choice."

How to Call for Help

If you or someone you know is suicidal, please, don't hesitate to call for help.

Click the following link to find the Suicide Hotline for your country.

http://ibpf.org/resource/list-international-suicide-hotlines

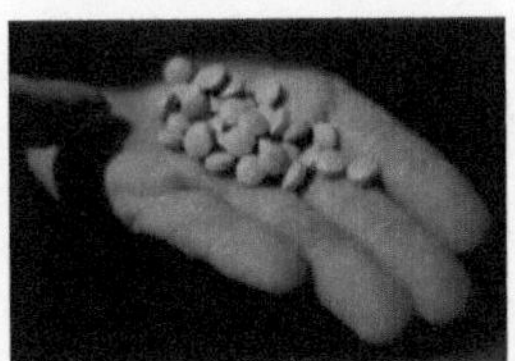

The Opioid Crisis in the United States: Who Is to Blame?

There can be no doubt that the United States is in the middle of a severe epidemic; opioid addiction and death. Once rare, drug-induced deaths from opioids has increased greatly over the past two decades killing more than 220,000 Americans between the years 1999-2017.

Recently big questions have been asked as to why we didn't see this coming and who is to blame. The answers to these questions have rocked the pharmaceutical world and made Americans rethink their trust in big pharma and the medical world.

How Big is the Problem?

The problem with opioids is huge with 60 people dying every day from overdoses. The stats are clear that 44 of those deaths are from prescription painkillers while 16 are from heroin.

The United States Centers for Disease Control (CDC), has made information available about the opioid crisis and its causes stating it has been caused and is continues to be fueled by the overprescribing of opioids for chronic pain.

Since the 1990s, big pharma has been pushing medications like OxyContin, Vicodin, Oxycodone, and Percocet and now the hens have come back to roost as 72,000 people in the United States have died in the past year by accidentally overdosing on opioids. All this just so that the owners of big pharma can continue to rake in billions of dollars every year.

Just in case you think I am exaggerating the danger and big pharma's sinister part in it, let's examine the facts.

Fact. Doctors and pharmaceutical corporations have been busy pushing the idea that opioids can be used safely and without addiction for decades. However, this isn't true. Yes, a person's history and the length of time opioids are used is vital in determining if you will get addicted and die limits these tragedies, however, there is no way for anyone to predict who will get hooked and who will not. Nor is it possible to say who will abuse their pain medicine and die.

Fact. Open Payments, a federal program that collects information on gifts given to doctors and teaching hospitals where a majority of the research is performed on opioids put out a report in 2005. It stated that $7.52 billion in gifts were given to physicians and teaching hospitals.

The result of all that money has been that doctors and researchers have been compliant with perpetuating myths founded questionable research findings.

Case and point. The misleading letter to the editor issued in 1980, by Jane Porter and Hershel Jick, M.D. from the Boston Collaborative Drug Surveillance Program at the Boston University Medical Center.

Porter and Jick had decided to find out if hospital patients receiving narcotics for pain in short-term treatment with opioids became addicted to them. They did so by reviewing the medical records of around 39,000 hospitalized patients. Nearly 12,000 of the patients they reviewed received narcotics while hospitalized, but only four developed an addiction.

Porter and Jick then reported their findings in a letter written to the editor of the New England Journal of Medicine.

The letter read in part:

"Recently, we examined our current files to determine the incidence of narcotic addiction in 39,946 hospitalized medical patients who were monitored consecutively. Although there were 11,882 patients who received at least one narcotic preparation, there were only four cases of reasonably well-documented addiction in patients who had no history of addiction. The addiction was considered major in only one instance.

The drugs implicated were meperidine in two patients. Percodan in one, and hydromorphone in one. We conclude that despite widespread use of narcotic drugs in hospitals, the development of addiction is rare in medical patients with no history of addiction."

Unfortunately, this letter to the editor was grasped by many people, including prescribing physicians, as proof that what big pharma had been telling them was true. Opioids were not dangerous and did not cause addiction. To make matters worse, the letter was cited 608 times and in 80% of those citations, the authors did not mention that the patients in the letter from Porter and Jick were in the hospital at the time of treatment.

Then in 1986, a study in the journal "Pain" reported they had observed 38 patients and concluded that opioid addiction was extremely rare. This backed up the letter to the editor of Porter and Jick giving a green light to advertise opioids as safe and effective.

The Opioid Crisis and Big Pharma

In 1996, the American Pain Society, a group of health care professionals and scientists were busy promoting changes in public policy and medical practices. In doing so, they declared that pain was the "fifth vital sign" and urged health care professionals to evaluate and address the pain of every patient upon their visit to the office.

There was one critical flaw in this thinking, pain is self-reported and cannot be tested for nor properly diagnosed.

This promotion to doctors that pain must be treated as a fifth vital sign in need of immediate consideration set the stage for the opioid crisis to begin.

Later in 1996, the huge corporation, Purdue Pharma released a new drug, an opioid called OxyContin. To increase sales, they released the video "I Got My Life Back" targeting prescribers. The video stated that opioid medications were the best pain medicines available and that they had few or no side effects. They went on to state, information straight from the osteoarthritis study, in the video that fewer than 1% of people who use opioids for pain develop addictions to them.

Then the drug companies launched an aggressive campaign of promoting their products using drug reps that were sent nationwide to doctors and clinics. They offered doctors gifts like expensive all-expense paid medical conferences if the doctor would visit the booth of the company at the conference.

Physicians and medical clinics were being bribed to prescribe opioid medications as the only pain remedies available and to support the claim that opioids are not addictive.

While the pharmaceutical companies were selling junk science to physicians, the medical schools in the United States were offering little or no training on the management of chronic pain. In fact, in 2010 it was reported that only 1 in 5 medical schools had any formal instruction on the topic.

In the void left by this lack of training pharmaceutical companies entered the picture, offering messages that stated opioids were without a doubt safe and effective.

The truth is that opioid painkillers aren't the only pain relievers available and they aren't safe.

The fact is that opioids aren't the only effective medications for chronic pain, they are only more aggressively marketed. It has been proven in study after study that over-the-counter medications such as Ibuprofen and Acetaminophen when given in combination might relieve pain much better than opioids. There are also drugs that help depression called SNRI's and some nerve medications like Gabapentin that were found to be effective against chronic pain as well.

The Dark History of Big Pharma and the Opioid Crisis

In 1995, the Food and Drug Administration (FDA) approved OxyContin permitting Purdue Pharma to claim that the drug was a long-acting formulation and was believed to reduce its abuse by drug abusers. This claim was based on the theory stated that drug abusers favored short-acting narcotics because they could get a faster "hit" than their product OxyContin would deliver.

So, it became the belief that drug abusers preferred short-acting painkillers like Percocet or Vicodin and would not abuse OxyContin.

Thus, Purdue Pharma used the FDA's decision as valuable and used it as their principal marketing tool.

In 2007, Purdue Pharma was confronted with evidence they had gathered that they had trained their sales representatives to tell doctors that OxyContin was less addictive than other opioids on the market.

The drug maker admitted summarily admitted the allegations. The report went on to state that because of their aggressive sales tactics, they had received approximately $2.8 billion in sales from OxyContin as of 2007.

More on this litigation later.

What Did Purdue Pharma Know About the Addictiveness of Their Product?

In 1998, just as OxyContin marketing was beginning to take off, Purdue Pharma received word that a study published in The Journal of Canadian Medical Association by researchers from the University of British Columbia in Vancouver was reporting that OxyContin was neither safe nor unattractive to drug abusers.

The study used interviews from local drug dealers and abusers to learn what prices legal drugs sold for on the black market. They found that MS Contin, another medication related to OxyContin that was also being aggressively marketed by Purdue Pharma was bringing a huge price for black marketers of the drug. A 30-milligram tablet that cost $1 at the pharmacy was demanding $40 on the street.

An editorial written by a Canadian physician, Dr. Brian Goldman stated that the findings of the report in the Journal of Canadian Medical Association should alert people to the idea that long-acting opioids like OxyContin were on their way to being highly "coveted" by drug dealers and users. In fact, he added in one paragraph that the study should "ring alarm bells."

However, Dr. Goldman was a paid speaker for Purdue Pharma and his "warning" wasn't meant to end widespread overprescribing of the pharmaceutical company's hit medication OxyContin. Instead, he went on in his editorial to state, "The publication of these findings will undoubtedly lead some to call for more action to stop the diversion of licit controlled substances.

But it's important not to overreact.

Although Sajan and colleagues have given us a fascinating window on the world of prescription drug diversion, their study provides no perspective on the scale of diversion, without which we risk overreacting to what may be an extremely limited phenomenon."

What happened to the study showing OxyContin is dangerous? Purdue Pharma did not alert either the FDA or its sales representatives that it existed. Instead, a sales official who worked for Purdue Pharma testified later to a federal grand jury that the company insisted that he distribute a different report that concluded that drug abusers were not at all attracted to time-release opioids.

In his testimony, Mr. Josephson, the above-mentioned Purdue Pharma sales official, stated that Purdue Pharma said it was not required that the drug company to tell the FDA about the Canadian study because the study was small and its results insignificant.

Misleading Information by Purdue Pharma Goes Big Time

As has already been starting, in December 1995 and going on until June 2001, Purdue supervisors and employees, meant to defraud. They marketed OxyContin as less addictive and less attractive to drug abusers.

These supervisors and employees then instructed Purdue Pharma sales reps to tell health care providers that Oxycodone was difficult for intravenous abusers to extract from OxyContin and thus was much less attractive to people who shot up drugs. They used Purdue's own study to show their reps and their customers that a drug abuser could extract only 68% of the Oxycodone from a single 10-milligram tablet by crushing it, stirring it into the water, and then drawing it through cotton into a syringe.

The problem with this claim is that OxyContin was distributed in 30-milligram tablets, not 10 as described in the study. The difference in the milligrams per tablet means a lot more could be extracted and abused.

They then told their sales reps to state to health care providers that OxyContin creates less chance for addiction than any other immediate-release opioids on the market at that time. They were also taught that the drug resulted in less euphoria and thus had a less potential for abuse.

Further, the company told some health care providers that they should not stop their patients from taking OxyContin abruptly as they would experience withdrawal symptoms.

The Osteoarthritis Drug Study

A study, drafted by some Purdue Pharma supervisors and employees then published in a medical journal in March 2000 claimed in the results section three misleading statements about the withdrawal syndrome and symptoms experienced by patients.

One. "One patient was hospitalized "for withdrawal symptoms…The patient who was hospitalized with withdrawal symptoms had completed the study on the previous day and had been receiving CR oxycodone, 70 mg/d; symptoms resolved after 3 days."

Two. "A second patient, who was receiving 60 mg/d CR oxycodone, experienced withdrawal symptoms after running out of study medication. The patient had not reported withdrawal symptoms during scheduled respites from doses of 30 or 40 mg/d."

Three. "Withdrawal syndrome was not reported as an adverse event for any patient during scheduled respites. Adverse experiences reported by more than 10% of patients during scheduled respites were nervousness (9 patients) and insomnia (8 patients)."

Since dubbed the osteoarthritis study, it also included the following information in its comment section to summarize the information given in the results section. It suggested that patients taking low doses could have their OxyContin treatment suddenly ended without experiencing withdrawal if their condition called for its discontinuance.

"There were 2 reports of withdrawal symptoms after patients abruptly stopped taking CR oxycodone at doses of 60 or 70 mg/d. Withdrawal syndrome was not reported as an adverse event during scheduled respites, indicating that {OxyContin] at doses below 60 mg (per day) can be discontinued without tapering the dose if the patient's condition so warrants."

From between June 2000 to June 2001 Purdue supervisors and employees distributed copies of the osteoarthritis study article widely, including to its sales representatives to use as marketing tools. They distributed 10,615 copies between February 2001 and June 2001 alone.

In June 2000, some Purdue Pharma supervisors and employees distributed the osteoarthritis study article with a marketing tip added to its sales force. The marketing tip that the pharmacy reps should use the reprint of the article as a tool for marketing success. With this tip came a list of 12 key points they were to use including:

"There were 2 reports of withdrawal symptoms after patients abruptly stopped taking CR oxycodone at doses of 60 or 70 mg/d. Withdrawal syndrome was not reported as an adverse event during scheduled respites indicating that CR oxycodone at doses below 60 mg. It can be discontinued without tapering the dose if the patient condition so warrants."

It is obvious that the pharmaceutical company wanted its salesforce and their customers to believe the lie that their product was safer and better than alternative treatments.

The Legal Action Taken Against Purdue Pharma

In 2001, Connecticut Attorney General Richard Blumenthal
announced that Purdue Pharma needed to take steps to end the
abuse of OxyContin. He went on to state in his statement that the
actions that had already been taken by Purdue Pharma were
"cosmetic and symbolic." He also noted after the pharmaceutical
company announced plans to reformulate the drug that the move
would take time, "Purdue Pharma has a moral, if not legal
obligation to take effective steps and address addiction and
abuse even as it works to reformulate the drug."

Then in 2004, West Virginia sued Purdue Pharma for
reimbursement of "excessive prescription costs." The state
claimed it had paid these funds because patients were taking
more of the drug than prescribed because the effects of the drug
wore off many hours before the twelve-hour threshold claimed
by the company.

West Virginia charged Purdue Pharma with deceptive marketing
and took them to court.

The judge wrote in his ruling that, "Plaintiff's evidence shows
Purdue could have tested the safety and efficacy of OxyContin at
eight hours, and could have amended their label, but did not."

This litigation never went before a jury and Purdue Pharma
agreed to settle, paying the state of West Virginia $10 million
for programs to help discourage abuse of their drugs.

It is interesting to note that all the evidence given during the
court hearing remains sealed by court order and is labeled
confidential.

In October 2007, it was Kentucky's turn to sue Purdue Pharma
for the widespread of abuse of OxyContin in Appalachia. The
suit demanded millions in compensation and eight years later
Purdue Pharma settled paying $24 million.

In 2007, The New York Times reported that Purdue Pharma had
been taken to federal court and charged with criminal misleading
of federal regulators, doctors, and patients about the risks of
addiction to OxyContin.

The parent company of Purdue Pharma pled guilty and was ordered to pay $600 million in fines and other payments. At the time, it was the of the largest amounts ever paid by a drug company in any related case. Also, three executives of Purdue Pharma pled guilty to the misbranding and criminal violation of federal laws and were ordered to pay a total of $34.5 million in fines.

The payments by Purdue Pharma and its employees totaled $634.5 million.

In the previous paragraph, I stated that Purdue Pharma had gained $2.8 billion in revenue from misleading the FDA, public, and physicians about OxyContin. I think it is obvious that the litigation brought in 2007 was only a slap on the wrist to Purdue Pharma.

Then in 2016, the Los Angeles Times reported that the 12-hour schedule told to patients by their doctors to adhere did not adequately control their pain resulting in withdrawal symptoms. The journalists concluded that this information gave, "new insight into why so many people have become addicted."

Using Purdue documents and other records, the L.A. Times claimed that Purdue Pharma was aware of this problem even before the drug went to market but "held fast to the claim of 12-hour relief, in part to protect its revenue [because] OxyContin's market dominance and its high price — up to hundreds of dollars per bottle — hinge on its 12-hour duration."

By that time OxyContin had become a hugely successful moneymaking drug as Purdue Pharma had increased its revenues from a few billion in 2007 to $35 billion by 2017. Then the famous magazine The New Yorker brought to light that Purdue Pharma is owned by one of America's richest families, the Sackler Family, with a net worth of $13 billion. The article's title is telling, "The Family that Built an Empire of Pain."

The article infuriated the public of the U.S. and people began to truly take note of the horrendous toll that addiction to the substance that had been marketed as safe was taking on innocent family and friends.

The straw that broke the proverbial camel's' back happened this year (2018), when Purdue Pharma patented and began marketing a new drug to control cravings to use in treating addictions to their own drug.

To date there are more than 16 lawsuits by states in the U.S. and Puerto Rico filed against Purdue Pharma and six other states Florida, Nevada, North Carolina, North Dakota, Tennessee, and Texas. All are charging Purdue Pharma for deceptive marketing practices and seeking damages.

The Real Question that Needs to Be Asked

The real question that needs to be asked is this, is big pharma the only reason for the epidemic of death in the US?

The answer is complicated, but I believe we are ALL to blame.

Although there can be no doubt that Purdue Pharma covered up the knowledge that OxyContin was a dangerous medication, corporations like Purdue Pharma pursue profits through the principal of supply and demand.

If people keep demanding their products, they will keep supplying to turn a profit.

It is true also that Purdue Pharma used deceptive marketing practices to sell their products and keep doctors prescribing by offering what amounts to bribes. But those same physicians had to notice that some of their patients were abusing their medications and hospitals also play a role as they did not report to the proper authorities the uptick they were experiencing in drug overdoses for a long time.

So, what can be done to end the opioid epidemic in the United States?

Across the country, there is a surge to work on strategies to end the opioid crisis. The United States Department of Health and Human Services has focused its efforts on five priorities:

1. Improve access to treatment and recovery services

2. Promoting the use of overdose-reversing drugs

3. Strengthening our understanding of the epidemic through better public health surveillance

4. Providing support for cutting-edge research on pain and addiction

5. Advancing better practices for pain management

While these are all noble goals, we are still missing one big piece of the puzzle to end the suffering of families who have lost to death someone they love from an opioid overdose. We need to find and implement non-drug ways treatments for chronic pain.

The journal <u>Pain Research and Treatment</u>, in May of this year (2018), reported on how useful and effective peripheral nerve stimulation is in treating chronic pain.

It's clear that as new technologies come into being, new treatments for chronic pain and many other disorders suffered by humanity will be found and utilized. The only things standing in the way of finding these better and non-addictive forms of help are the wars being waged by big corporations like Purdue Pharma and the American people who believe that a pill can solve every problem.

It is my sincere hope that you will consider the words written here in this report and heed my warning against overuse of prescription painkillers. It only takes a few days of using these strong medications to become hopelessly addicted, so if it is at all possible, avoid using opioids.

The quality of your life and the possibility of your death from overdose hang in the balance.

Life Isn't Easy, Life Isn't Fair

There are two basic facts about life that many people either were never taught or they try to say do not apply to themselves: Life isn't easy, and life isn't fair. These two concepts are true for everyone, no matter your financial status, your ethnic background, your sexual orientation, or your religious affiliation.

Yet, we expend a lot of energy fighting against these unavoidable realities. I shall endeavor in this piece to explain these two facts in a way that makes sense, and the benefits of learning to live with them instead of trying to fight against them, a battle that simply cannot be won.

LIFE ISN'T EASY

No matter who you are, life isn't easy. From our first breath, we struggle to get our needs met. We must cry and coo to get our parents to give us our most basic necessities and we learn very early that we will not always get what we want, no matter how badly we act out. The despair we feel when we realize this truth is only compounded if the people we should be able to count on for our needs are abusive or neglectful. We grow up feeling rejected and unworthy of even taking up space in the world. Somehow that angst leads to us growing into adults who feel that the world owes us a living, so we set out to force it to pay us and we withdrawal into our own inner worlds. The result is that no matter which direction we go, we end up hiding from any hope of happiness choosing instead to keep our misery going.

When I entered therapy almost 28 years ago, I felt extreme anger at the harshness of the life I had been dealt. It was hell going to therapy every week and facing head-on the facts of what had been my childhood, and I was furious about it. I felt that had my family of origin been "normal" I wouldn't have been having to fight so hard to recover. I spent many hours in my therapist's office weeping and moaning about how hard life was and how I had been cheated. One day my therapist looked at me and said words that have made a huge change in how I see the world.

"Shirley, life isn't easy for anyone. Granted, most people do not have to live with the amount of stuff you survived, but that's comparing apples to oranges. No one, and I mean no one, has it easy in life. That is an inevitable fact we all must live with."

At first, I was angry at her. I felt like I deserved to be pissed and that life should be easy for me after all I had been through. After a time, after I had mulled those words over and over in my mind, I began to understand. I had been spending so much time feeling like I was owed something from the world that I had forgotten to live. Life, I have begun to understand, is beautiful BECAUSE it isn't easy.

LIFE ISN'T FAIR

This concept is one that takes some choking to get down.

Here again, we face something that most humans just don't want to understand, let alone accept. The inevitable truth that life isn't fair for anyone, and that we must accept the things we cannot change. It grates against all our human need to control every aspect of our existence.

There are three areas of our lives that are totally out of our control.

- We cannot control other people.

- We cannot change the past.

- We all will die someday.

Like my brother stated earlier today when describing his
frustration with his life, "There is a little kid inside me who
wants to stomp and scream!" I think we can all relate to his
statement. Inside of us all is a part who is angry as hell because
we can't control the three things listed above, especially our
inability to change other people.

I spent a lot of energy on these thoughts, ranting and raging
because, "Dammit, why should I have to pay for the actions of
my abusers? Why do I have to pay a therapist and live through
this hell because of what they did? I robbed of a normal
childhood, and the joy of living happily ever after!!!!"

Here again I got stuck for a while.

After I had been in recovery for around 24 years, I had come to
believe I was doing very well and had accepted life on life's
terms. Then tragedy struck, not once, but twice. My little
nephew Jimmy was stillborn and only a few months later I was
diagnosed with breast cancer and had to undergo two disfiguring
surgeries. I became betrayed and angry at life. I felt like I had
paid my dues and that it was time that I enjoyed some good
times, and I couldn't reconcile the crap that I was having to face.
To make matters even worse, my best friend of 27 years died the
following spring. I had come so far, surviving not only my
horrific childhood, but also living through the dangerous pitfalls
of therapy, and now this?

Again, it was my therapist who helped me to learn another very
important lesson. After listening to me bellyache for the two-
hundredth time about how unfair it all was to me, she sat back
and after making sure she had my full attention spoke more
words of wisdom.

"Shirley, people are born and people die. People get sick and
they get well. People come into our lives, and they depart. Did
you think you were alone in these truths? No Shirley. Life isn't
fair. It is messy and full of hardships, and you know what else?
You will someday die, just like everyone else, including myself.
To allow yourself to fall victim to becoming bitter because you
are just like the rest of us is to allow yourself to be cheated."

After digesting her words, I soon realized she was correct. I had
been seeing life as a child sees it, as either being good or bad,
when in reality, it is neither. Life is life, no more, no less. We
can either get busy enjoying it and stop trying to force it to be
what it is not, or we can get busy allowing our preconceived
notions of what it SHOULD BE destroy us.

NOPE, LIFE ISN'T EASY, AND LIFE ISN'T FAIR.

We set ourselves up for disappointment when we don't accept
these two premises. We waste valuable time we could be
spending enjoying the things in life that make living worthwhile.
I've discovered that I am my own worst enemy in this. There is
no one abusing or neglecting me today, the only person who
harms me now is myself.

I have decided to let go, as much as is humanly possible, of the
notion that the world owes me anything and that life should be
fair and easy. The frustration that I have been experiencing all
my life has dropped a substantial amount since I've been
working on these concepts. I try to not expect people or life to
treat me the way I want to be treated and, in this way that little
child in me gets to take a rest from having her temper tantrum
whenever I hit a snag.

Life is busy, hazardous, hard, beautiful and only is issued to
each of us once. Why squander it bemoaning what we don't
have? Why not enjoy every moment as though it were our last?
Yes, hard times will come, but we can gain some measure of
comfort in knowing that this is the same fate of all of mankind.

I have decided to live. How about you?

"Life is what we make it, always has been, always will be."
Grandma Moses

The Invisible Child

I am facing my forty-year graduating class anniversary dinner in August. Such an event usually causes people to look forward to speaking with and seeing the people with which you went to school.

For me the prospect brings back memories and emotions that are not lovely.

I can remember moving to Illinois from Tennessee when I was a little older than eight. We moved here in the spring of 1968 a few months before mankind took its first giant leap onto the moon's surface. I was content at first, but we had moved to within a fifteen-minute drive of one of the people who traumatized me in childhood.

The Maltreatment Escalated

In the fall of 1968, I began attending Lincoln grade school. As if moving to Illinois with its corn fields and bean fields wasn't enough of a shock, attending school certainly was much more so.

Not only were there no African-American children in my school, even the janitors and lunch ladies were white. The children seemed different too. I can't explain exactly what I meant, except to say they were crueler than those I had left behind in Shelby County Tennessee.

It was only the first day of school when the teasing began. I spoke with a heavy southern accent and the kids picked up on that quickly. To make matters worse, in the fourth grade I began to develop breasts and a girlish figure which made the other little girls laugh. I don't know if they were laughing in jealousy or because they didn't understand. Either way, their giggles seared my soul.

Even though I was laughed at and ridiculed, I still could surf the waves of disappointment and homesickness.

The homesickness was Dreadful

I would sit upstairs in our little house on Marshall Avenue and daydream of moving home to Tennessee. I couldn't stand the idea that I was going to have to live out my life among the cruel Yankee children I had encountered.

Also, I had never slept at night, but my insomnia became even worse in Illinois.

My father knew I was miserable and that I wanted to move back to Tennessee. It hurt him that he couldn't fulfill his little girl's wish, but he was powerless to do anything about it. Although he had served his country during the Viet Nam War in the Navy, he was penniless and had been forced to relocate his family in Illinois where he had been raised. He had hoped to offer us some sense of stability, not understanding he was dooming us to poverty and despair.

I spent the fourth grade at Lincoln grade school spending most of my time switching from one alter to another and trying my best to get by. My teachers thought I was a daydreamer because I paid so little attention in class. I was mentally present only part of the time and I was bored. I found the lessons in math and reading in Illinois boring compared to the classes I had attended in Tennessee.

Shortly after I completed fourth grade, we moved to a little town nearby. The person who did perhaps the most damage to my young mind and body lived on the other side of a fence of our backyard. As one might suspect, the traumatic injuries increased by multitudes. It was while living there that my first neck injury occurred when I was throttled for not cooperating.

By the time we moved back to town, my mental health was in shambles. I was eleven-years old and had already made the decision to never play again with other children again. That decision isolating me from any hope of having friends.

Becoming Invisible

Luckily most of the children in my sixth-grade class were easy to get along with. They only teased me mercilessly when the rare occasions came for me to kick a ball during a game. Most of the time I maneuvered myself successfully out of that situation though by becoming invisible.

Oh, I don't mean physically and literally invisible. But if I stood about quietly and was careful, I would be passed over by a turn at bat unnoticed by the teachers at P.E.

It wasn't long before I was utilizing this ability in all my encounters with people. Not just kids and teachers at school, but also with relatives and friends.

The problem with being invisible is that no one can hear or see your distress.

When I entered puberty, which for me came early, I became more and more depressed. I often contemplated death by suicide and was suffering at the hands of a person I loved very much.

To this day I cannot understand why he would want to hurt me like that. I loved him so much. It was so unnecessary.

An invisible person cannot tell you they are hurting. I suffered in silence, praying to die.

The bullying at school grew. I had the air of a person who was bleeding, and like chickens, peck at blood, so did the kids.

Looking back, I can see that what the kids were doing wasn't meant to be as cruel as I perceived at the time. The things they were saying should have been laughed at and not have been so devastating. But I was in too much pain. My heart was broken and bruised so I took every little tease to heart.

When I was fifteen the unspeakable happened. My 39-year old father dropped dead of a heart attack in front of myself, my two brothers and my mother in our kitchen.

My only hope of going back to Tennessee also died that day.

I Hated Illinois

Oh God how I hated Illinois.

I felt I had been robbed of my life and by this midwestern state, and now it had taken my father from me too.

It was only a few short months later that I told on the man whom I had loved and who had so horribly harmed me all my life.

 Things did not go well.

When I was taken to confront him directly with my accusations, he not only denied doing anything wrong, but said, and I quote, "How could you say those things about me?"

I became an outcast of those people related to the man that day.

The entire lot of them, except one brave soul, discarded me like yesterday's garbage. They did this to a fifteen-year old girl who had just lost her father, and whom they knew was telling the truth.

I became even more invisible as this man's wife would bring presents for my brothers but not me. I never received another birthday card or acknowledgement of being alive from people who had once meant the world to me.

To this day, I cannot stand the thought of being in the same room with them. I don't identify anyone anymore in my writing to protect the people who were innocent children at the time, but I have no love for the lot of them.

Being an Invisible Human Being Hurts

No one can love you if you can't be seen.

No one can help you navigate life or teach you how to live if they cannot see you.

So, when I received the invitation to my forty-year class graduation party, I almost said no. The old anger resurfaced with force and I strung a long list of curse words in describing the people of that class. Facing those people who were around when all this pain was happening seemed to be a bigger trigger than I could face.

Then I thought on in harder and in a clearer manner.

It is not the fault of the people with whom I graduated that my life was so horrendous. They were just kids too. I have gone as far as going down a different aisle in a grocery store to not speak to any of them for many years. It's time to lay the illusion that it was their fault to rest.

They were just kids. They had no idea what horrible maltreatment I was enduring, nor were they at all responsible for it. The dissociative disorder I developed also was not their fault. I used my hate for them as a cover for where that anger and resent belonged, on the adults who were hurting me.

Nor was the state of Illinois' fault.

No matter where I had lived as a kid, my life had been full of trauma and a geographical move did not make it worse. It just changed the dynamics of what was happening.

The man who hurt me here came to Tennessee on visits on a regular basis and the DID I now live with began to form in infancy not after the move.

Never Again

I guess the biggest reason I write this blog is to not be invisible anymore. I fight myself constantly to get out and be noticed in public. Being physically out in public is extremely trying and tiring for me. Yet, I go out anyway and speak and write about my traumatic history.

Why?

I don't want any other people who experience being invisible as children. I want to shout from the rooftops that childhood trauma is preventable and unnecessary.

I feel the need to raise awareness in the public's eye that we must not avoid discussing what happens to children every day in the world.

My message is simple. Children are being harmed in your community, in your neighborhood, and possibly in your family.

No one is immune, and everyone is responsible for these unspeakable crimes that are committed every day against the most innocent among us, our kids.

Right now, I am appalled at what is happening to the children who are being ripped from their mothers and fathers at the southern border of my country. We are all complacent with bullying and child abuse on a massive scale that has been sanctioned by my government.

Oh god, every time I read a new headline about that atrocity, I wish I could be invisible again.

But to become invisible and not be noticed is to do what my adults did to me, keep quiet even when we know for certain a child is being harmed.

I do not want to be invisible anymore. No, never again.

"I like to be left alone

But when people don't notice I'm

Absent

It hurts

And I know it's my own fault

For becoming invisible

For isolating myself

But just once I want someone to

Notice

To truly notice and care"

~ G.P.

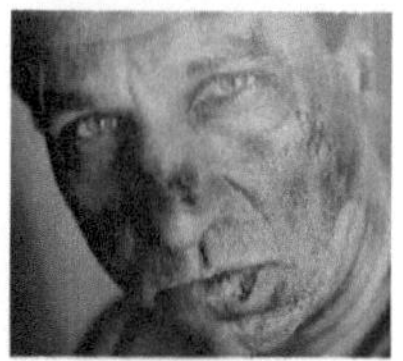

Our Men Aren't Okay

Women have been rightfully marching together protesting the way we have been treated down through history. We women have received less pay, been forced to do menial labor and expected to raise children alone all while being vilified.

However, from my last post, it's clear that men, like women, are often victims of childhood and adult trauma. In that post, I wrote about how men have been forgotten in the #MeToo movement.

Today I want to address the largest obstacle men face and how it is killing them by the millions. The stresses that society presses upon them that are both unfair and unreachable.

The Facade of Strength

While women have indeed been victims of injustice and inequality, men have also been victims. Men are expected to look, feel, and above all be strong. We measure a man's worth as a society by looking at his job, his prowess with the ladies, and his ability to be #1.

The result of these societal pressures is that men are forced to play a terrible game. They must put on a façade of "I'm Okay" when they are not.

The proof that men aren't okay lies in the following statistics. Although women are three times more likely to attempt to die by suicide, men are almost four times more likely to succeed.

If you think that sounds bad, read these further stats from the Centers for Disease Control (CDC).

• Males take their own lives at nearly four times the rate of females and represent 77.9% of all suicides.
• Suicide is the seventh leading cause of death for men
• Firearms are the most commonly used method of suicide among males (56.9%).
• 95% of the prison population are men.
• 73% of adults who go missing are men.

What is the catalyst for these atrocious statistics?

I believe, and there is research to back up my assumption, that the number one reason men are deciding to die before their time is directly related to the unfair expectation's society has of who they are and how they should perform.

Indeed, the CDC also reported that the men who died by suicide were not diagnosed with a mental health condition. The reasons for our men dying include perceived weaknesses in themselves from relationship problems, money/legal problems, substance abuse, and physical health problems.

A New Word for You Today: Misandry

Most of us, especially in the wake of the #MeToo movement, have heard the term misogyny: the dislike, contempt for or ingrained prejudice against women.
Don't get me wrong, misogyny is alive and well in society today. Women are less likely to be appointed to high-paying executive jobs and draw lower salaries than men.

However, how many of you have heard the term misandry?

I found the best definition and explanation of misandry on Wikipedia:

"Misandry is the hatred of, contempt for, or prejudice against men or boys. Misandry can manifest itself in numerous ways, including sexual discrimination, denigration of men, violence against men, and sexual objectification of men."

It used to be that misandry was underground and women showed their contempt for men behind closed doors and only to other women. I know I have been guilty of saying a few of the following phrases that are misandrous in nature, how about you?

• "Men only think with their dicks."
• "A man wouldn't understand."
• "Men just want a hole to put it in."
• "Men can't hear the word no." (when rejected sexually)

We, women, spend a lot of time complaining about how we have been treated, yet if men stood up, (and some have), to ask that their need for respect be met, we women tend to stare at them and think very unkind thoughts about them (to put it mildly).

However, now misandry has moved into the public domain as women react to the bad treatment they have received from men.

To be honest, many people, both men, and women do not understand they are saying or acting in a misandrous manner. Society has set up men for a perfect storm of being human but not being able to act on their human emotions or frailties.

Obviously, men are not so strong that they cannot experience extreme emotional distress. However, men are very reluctant to reach out for help. The answer to the puzzle of why men don't reach out is plainly seen in society's unreal and unreachable expectations of them.

Men Must Be the Breadwinners

How a man makes his money is the number one question people ask men. We don't ask how their health is or how their children are doing in school, we ask them about their job and their wages.

Not only is asking such a question extremely rude, but it also traps men into believing they must either lie or feel shame if they cannot answer the way society expects them to.

My brother has a very serious anxiety disorder brought on by the actions of our narcissistic and abusive mother. He has not been able to keep a job for more than a few weeks or months at a time. He has held over one-hundred positions, but his anxiety attacks soon begin, and he is forced to leave work.

So, when he attends a public function and is asked about where he is working, he is overwhelmed with shame that he does not deserve.

Society has decided that a man's worth lies directly in line with his bank account, his level of education, how many hours he works a week, and the type of car he drives.

Men Must Not Be Stay at Home Dads

In 2013, the U.S. Census Bureau reported that there was 214,000 stay at home dads in the United States.

The Census also gave a definition of what was meant by an at-home dad:

The U.S. Census defines "at-home dad" as a father not in the labor force for the past 52 weeks and whose wife was in the labor force for the past 52 weeks.

The bureau also did not consider a man a stay at home father if he is looking for work or going to school or if the spouse is out of work to change jobs for a week or more.

However, as an article from The Good Men Project points out, not all the stay at home dads out there were counted. They argue that the census misses:

"all the dads out there who are working out of the home, either full or part-time; who are hanging a shingle as a consultant, a freelancer, or a landscaper; who work three nights a week part-time at the restaurant down the street; or any of the dads out there who are actively looking for full-time work.

While dads may be serving as the primary caregiver for their kids or sharing a substantial part of the parenting load, the Census simply does not count them as full-time dads—even though it's more than a full-time occupation."
Why the discrepancy? What could be causing the problem with how the United States Census Bureau defines a stay at home dad?

The answer is clear, society refuses to allow men to fulfill any other role as the father of his children than breadwinner and disciplinarian.

On an even more bizarre note, society also believes that all men are oddballs and cannot change a diaper, keep a house clean or even wear matching pairs of clean socks. Men are also believed to be incapable of cooking, combing the hair of their little girls or giving their children the warmth and compassion, they need.

To make matters even worse, many people also feel that to stay at home to care for your family is the ultimate womanizing of men that somehow makes them less masculine.

How sad.

Also, even though women are also known to be perpetrators of sexual violence against children, when men take their children to the playground they report being eyed with suspicion by the mothers they encounter.

One man's account I read, stated that when he would go to the park with his little girl, the women who were there with their children refused to even acknowledge his offers of "good morning" opting instead to glare at him.

Misandry and the Value of Men's Lives

In the era of #MeToo, it is incredible to think about how we value men's lives as disposable.

To show you how much we value men's less than women's, read to this quote from Social Psychologist Professor Roy F. Baumeister.

"When the news media report some disaster, they sometimes use the phrase 'even women and children' if such are among the victims. The phrase expresses the point that men's lives are valued less [than] anyone else's life.

This attitude helps to remind each man that, in a desperate situation, he is expected to give up his life quickly and readily and without complaint, if doing so will save a woman or child.

One of the most famous disasters of the twentieth century was the sinking of the Titanic. [The life-boat] seats were given to the women, while the men stayed on board to drown."

Did you feel a twinge of anger while reading the above quote? Was your anger pointed at the fact that the lives of men are considered less valuable than women, or pointed at Professor Baumeister for his insight and myself for quoting him?

Please, take a hard look at your own attitude, I know I had to my own.

Men Must Not Only Be Competitive, They Must Also Be Winners

Society believes that all men MUST always be striving to be better than other men. They should compete in sports in High School, watch football, and above all "score" with as many women as possible.

The truth is much different. Although it is hard to get them to admit it in public, men need and crave compassion, understanding, love, and respect just as much and sometimes more than women.

Practically from the day of a man's birth, he is filled with the message that he must win. We buy new baby boy's footballs and dream of our sons playing for the NFL where he will win, win, win!

They become indoctrinated quickly to the notion that they are to use their penis as a weapon to get their way and some take that to the extreme resulting in date rape. Then when forced to take a hard at themselves for what they have done, society comes to their defense saying that "men always think with their little heads."

There is an ongoing psychological debate over what makes human beings tick. Is it nature, the belief that our genetic makeup, i.e. our sexuality as determined by our genes? Or nurture, how we are raised that makes us who we are as people?

I argue that while men are genetically destined to be stronger and bigger than most women, it is only when they are told they are dominant over females that they come to act out what is expected of them.

In short, the violence of men is directly proportional to what they are taught by parents, teachers, and society as a whole.

Men are Victims of Violence Too

Violence isn't just happening to women in America, it also happens to men. Attacks from other men and the women they become intimately involved with happen every day.

To understand what I am talking about, read on.

The National Domestic Violence Hotline statistics prove that women are not the only victims of rape, physical violence or stalking by an intimate partner in the United States.

While nearly 3 in 10 women (29%) are experiencing rape, physical violence or stalking, 1 in 10 men (10%) do as well.

In fact, 1 in 4 women (24.3%) and 1 in 7 men (13.8%) aged eighteen years and older have been victims of severe violence.

Then there is this statistic where women and men are even in experiencing psychological aggression (48.4% and 48.8% respectively.)

If you found those stats hard to swallow, then hold onto your hat for this next one because it is shocking and not at all pretty.

According to a paper first published in 2015 in the journal Psychological Services, 50% of our armed service members who were raped serving our country were male.

So, what happens if you a male and have been raped by your Commanding Officer or by one of the other men in your unit? Do you go to the nearest hospital to report a rape? Do you tell someone?

The answer to both questions is no. A man who admits to being raped by another man would be emasculated by the other men in his unit and receive enormous ridicule.

It is no wonder that men choose to die by suicide.

The humiliation they face is tremendous and unforgiving. And, if you are thinking these rapes are being committed by gay men serving in the military, you would be dead wrong.

Rape is never about sex, it's about power. The power to control someone else's terror and will. There is no other less powerful position in the world than being a new recruit in the military.

New recruits are stripped of their own thinking power and are not allowed to question authority. These parameters can set up men in uniform for the perfect storm as a heterosexual commander may demand and then receive sexual favors of the men and women under his command.

Then in a twisted side-effect, the commander's behavior is mimicked by service members who outrank new recruits.

The message the military and their commanding officers send is loud and clear; I totally own you.

Pulling it All Together

As a woman myself, I completely understand why women have been so militant in this era of #MeToo, I wanted to give a glimpse at the other side of the coin.

Yes, women have been victims of men in terms of them lording over us for millennia, however, should we behave the same way towards them?

In vilifying every man in the nation, are we not throwing out the baby with the bathwater as it were? Turning a blind face to the pain and discomfort men endure daily?

I put it to you that men matter and if we are to grow up as a society we must band together, people of all races, and yes, sexes to make the world safer for all of us.

The next time you hear someone or yourself, say something cruel about a man, rethink what you are doing.

It will take all of us to change the world, men included.

Women Sexual Abusers of Children; The Silent Crisis

I realize just the title of this blog post will turn people away, they can't or won't read what I have to say on this subject.

However, the problem with sticking our head in the sand attitude is that a problem that is not acknowledged is not solvable. Any recovering alcoholic or drug addict will tell you, the first step in defeating a problem, is to admit that it exists.

Although It Is Hard, We Must End the Abuse of Our Children

I know, this is hard to talk about, but we must band together to find a way to end this hideous blight on our society.

Some might even be thinking, "What's the problem with women molesting children anyway? Won't the kids outgrow and forget what happened when they are older?

Surely women can't harm children as much as men! I mean, they don't have penises, so they can't penetrate the girls or make the boys give them oral sex, so how much harm can they really be doing?"

Those beliefs, that children cannot be harmed by a woman sexual predator are not only alarming, but they are also universal. To make matters worse, there are many who refuse to believe that a mother would ever perform sex or request sex from their own children. Unfortunately, this last belief is the most damaging to children who are being harmed.

The Statistics of Female Child Predators are Staggering and Sobering

In the stats laden paragraph below, we will examine the number of women perpetrators of sexual abuse in the United States.

While numbers are huge, they only based on the people who got caught and does not include the crimes where victims remained and still remain silent.

According to Stats of Victims of Child Sexual Abuse 14% of boys and 6% of girl victims of sexual abuse were abused by female perpetrators. Also, according to the website Child Molestation and Prevention: 1/20 men and 1/3300 women are child sexual predators.

Then, U.S. Census Bureau Quick Facts, one can see that the total population of the US as of 2015 is 323,127,513 people. 63.3% were adults over the age of 18; 50.8% of the adult population of the US were female; 49.2% of the adult population of the US are male.

That means that in 2015, 164,148,777 adult women in the US and 158,978,736 adult men.

Statistically speaking, 49,742 women perpetrators of sexual abuse, usually against their own children.

The Smallest Victims of Sexual Violence by Women

Now we shall examine together the staggering number of girls and boys who are the victims of female predators.

The Child Data Center tables show that the number of children in the US in 2015 was 118,587,798 with 51% of these children being male 49% of these children being female.

Breaking it down by the numbers, there were 60,479,777 were little boys and 58,108,021 little girls.

From using the stats above we can calculate that in 2015, there was a real possibility that 3,682,786 little boys and 3,486,481 little girls were molested in 2015 by female predators.

That means there is a high probability that 49,742 women in the year 2015 were sexually abusing children, usually their own.

Adding the two figures together, 7,169,267 children of either sex are molested sexually, by a female perpetrator in 2015 in the United States alone.

Why Do Perpetrators Commit Acts of Sexual Violence Against Children

A high percentage of men who were studied were abused by female sexual predators and became abusers themselves.

In the journal *The Future of Children* in the summer/autumn edition of 1994, Princeton University reported on a research project they had conducted to summarize other papers to find the immediate and long-term impacts on children who are sexually abused. This resource found staggering information about the long-term effects of child molestation.

I quote their abstract and their findings below:

"Research conducted over the past decade indicates that a wide range of psychological and interpersonal problems are more prevalent among those who have been sexually abused than among individuals with no such experiences. Although a definitive causal relationship between such difficulties and sexual abuse cannot be established using current retrospective research methodologies, the aggregate of consistent findings in this literature has led many to conclude that childhood sexual abuse is a major risk factor for a variety of problems.

"This article summarizes what is currently known about these potential impacts of child sexual abuse.

"The various problems and symptoms described in the literature on child sexual abuse are reviewed in a series of broad categories including posttraumatic stress, cognitive distortions, emotional pain, avoidance, an impaired sense of self, and interpersonal difficulties.

"Research has demonstrated that the extent to which a given individual manifests abuse-related distress is a function of an undetermined number of abuse-specific variables, as well as individual and environmental factors that existed prior to, or occurred subsequent to, the incidents of sexual abuse."

So, current research has found a direct link between men who grow up to become sexual predators and those who have been sexually molested in their own childhood by a female relative.

Findings suggested that female sex offenders had a high incidence of:

- Alcohol and drug use

- Severe mental health problems

- Learning disabilities

- Physical health problems

Furthermore, the presence of domestic violence in the home increased the likelihood of a female being listed as the primary perpetrator by almost two and a half times.

Female sexual offenders present as a group of people dealing with:

- Complex layers of trauma

- Disability

- Illness

- Vulnerability

There are also some conditions that exacerbate the problem, mainly centering around inappropriate boundary development for the woman and the child.

It is also true that a high percentage of women were abused by female sexual predators and became abusers themselves.

Female Sexual Predation Has Been Overlooked for Far Too Long

For far too long, people including law enforcement have been reluctant to discuss female predation against children. However, this is slowly changing.

A paper published in the Journal of Sexual Abuse in 2015, is part of the burgeoning movement to understand female predation.

Using research gathered from 2010, the paper struggles to identify the differences between male and female predators and why women often go undetected.

The researchers discovered that largely due to a failure of society to recognize women as offenders, the United States has allowed them to avoid detection, prosecution, and interventions such as tracking, offender registration and mandated treatment for sexual predators.

They also stated a possible reason:

"This [difference in treatment between male and female perpetrators] could be partially due to differences that exist in their offending behaviors, victim profiles, and personal characteristics that set them apart from male offenders, to whom our systems have become more attuned."

When the researchers studied the data from Child Protective Services in the U.S., they found that slightly over 20% of substantiated child sexual abuse that was reported to authorities involved only a female perpetrator. That is one out of every five.

However, when the female perpetrator was not the only person involved but had a partner that number jumps to over 42%.

Women perpetrators also showed a distinct preference toward female victims over male, by 68% choosing to abuse their own daughters over others but not limited to only their daughters. Indeed, their findings indicated that female perpetrators were more likely to commit sexual crimes if they are the parent of the victim (77.8%).

That means that when the perpetrator was a biological parent, the data showed the researchers that the offender was over four and a half times more likely to be female.

The Effects from Childhood Sexual Trauma that Carry into Adulthood

Adults who have experienced child sexual trauma grow up to have a myriad of emotional problems and relationship difficulties. Below I've outlined only a few of the effects adults experience directly a result of early childhood sexual trauma.

Self-Esteem issues. The survivor may feel a sense of hopelessness, helplessness and like they don't belong in the world. They may have a deep sense that their birth was a mistake, and they should die. They may see themselves as unworthy of any good things, and either they will isolate away from others, or they will feel so needy they will be in one relationship after another.

Post-Traumatic Stress Disorder. This disorder cannot be pushed under the rug as unimportant. People who live with its effects can tell you it is misery. The things done to survivors when they are children CANNOT and WILL NOT be forgotten by them when they are adults. Perhaps they may have suppressed the memories of the molestation, but somewhere in their brain is burned the details of the emotions and feelings they felt while the perpetrator was harming them. These memories surface in nightmares, flashbacks, and dissociation.

Depression. People who have been sexually molested as children are four times more likely to be diagnosed with major depression. Depression is no joke, and it cannot be cured by just forcing themselves to get better. It is a serious and potentially deadly problem. The internal conflicts brought on by feelings of guilt and rage about their being sexually used by someone who was supposed to be their caregiver is enormous. If not treated, many will die by suicide.

Dissociative Disorders. These disorders include depersonalization, derealization, and at the far extreme of the spectrum, dissociative identity disorder. Living with a dissociative disorder is horrific. Many lose time, don't remember important events and have a severely altered sense of identity.

Problems in relationships. Both men and women who were abused by women perpetrators suffer from isolation. Yes, they may have been married once or a dozen times, but because they lack the skills to relate to their partners, these relationships do not last. They sometimes prefer to be alone rather with other people, because they feel safer alone.

Anxiety Disorders. Because sexual abuse is threatening and disruptive, children often develop a sense of insecurity and don't believe the world is a safe place. This belief system expresses itself in adulthood as anxiety. One is hyperalert and afraid of things that others don't notice. This anxiety can manifest itself as panic attacks in adulthood. These overwhelming attacks make the person feel like they are going to die or that they have lost their mind.

Anger issues. Children who have been molested by their female caregivers may be left in adulthood with extreme anger issues. Although the person who harmed them may no longer be alive, the anger persists and can spill out into the survivor's home and work life.

Child Molestation is Tragic

As you can clearly see, molestation by women not only exists, it is a tragic crime that leaves children hopeless to grow up to be neurotic and disturbed adults.

This is a tragedy that must stop. So long as we, as a society, continue to ignore the fact that women can and do indeed, harm children by sexually abusing them, this crime will go on and future generations will suffer.

Please, help the children. Stop child abuse in any form in its tracks by acting. If you see or suspect a child of being molested by either a man or a woman, ***DO NOT remain silent***.

Speak up for that child's safety.

If you are wrong and what you saw is innocent, then deal with that later. The welfare of that child is and should be your primary concern. You can apologize later.

The children of the United States are its future, and we will be judged by how we manage or don't, this silent crisis.

"Our lives begin to end the day we become silent about things that matter."

~ Martin Luther King Jr.

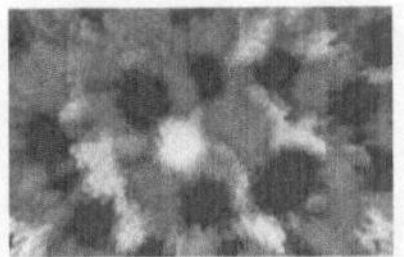

The Power of Fusion

In this article, I would like to discuss with you the final stage of integration, fusion.

There is a lot of resistance to this stage among the DID community, but there need not be.

Hopefully, by the end of this article, you will have a better understanding of fusion and feel more capable of working towards this important step towards ending the chaos that comes from remaining fragmented.

The Fragmented Self

Upon entering therapy, multiples begin traveling the long road of self-discovery of not only our pasts but also who we are in all our incarnations. We learn our alters names, their preferences, and the memories of what we endured that caused them to form.

To be sure, we owe our alternate selves our deepest respect and love because, without their existence, we could not have survived with our bodies and minds intact. They took the brunt of the fear and pain that was inflicted upon our bodies and minds when we were too young to defend ourselves.

However, it is also vital to understand that the alters in our fragmented minds are not strangers or even separate people. They are us and we are them.

The Chaos from Being Fragmented

I don't think any person with the diagnosis of dissociative identity disorder would deny that being fragmented is very chaotic. Money, clothes and even relationships come and go as the alters in our systems ebb and flow.

I have had more than my fair share of chaos from being fragmented, as I have been accused of doing and saying many things down through my adult life.

Once I was told by a woman friend I worked with that I had threatened to kill her. After my actions, she would have nothing to do with me any longer.

I once woke up married to a man I barely knew and remained with him for over eight years because I felt obligated to do so.

I have also broken the law and had to sit in the police station pondering when and how I had done what they said.

These and events like them, are only some of the reasons I sought to end the chaos and literally pull myself together as closely as humanly possible.

I sought and worked towards fusion.

The Fourth Stage of Integration: Fusion

As I have written in a previous post (see it here), a lot of multiples are afraid of even discussion of integration let along its final stage fusion.

I think a lack of information on what fusion entails is probably the main reason why. In fact, if you google fusion as a stage of healing in therapy with dissociative identity disorder, you'll find very few choices.

Unfortunately, many of those choices you do find during a google search on fusion are written by people who haven't lived through the process themselves. This lack of first-hand information means google will bring up several conflicting explanations and misinterpretations.

Fusion, simply put, means accepting the alters in your system as parts of you but also beginning to think, speak and act as one person instead of many.

You incorporate all the wonderful parts of yourself that were never allowed to coalesce into one personality. Their talents, memories and skills and yours, merge as closely as possible to form one vital entity.

You also take full responsibility for your actions even if you should dissociate due to stress and no longer make statements such as, "she did that" or "he did this."

Fusion does not mean the disappearance or death of the alters. The only reason I can say that is because doing either is impossible. The alters are you and you are the alters. If one dies, so do all of you. You are and will be together forever.

Fusion is NOT Becoming a Singleton it is Something Else

Fusion is not becoming a singleton, that is also impossible.

I have explained in other posts (see it here), during early childhood (usually agreed the age of 5) there is a stage when the personality of children coalesce was missed by people living with dissociative identity disorder. Our brains have been altered in structure and cannot re-enter the missed developmental stage and become one cohesive entity.

However, we can progress through the four stages of integration to become close, if not perfectly, to an approximation of being one whole person.

Fusion, as I have been experiencing it, means growing closer and closer to my alters and the gaps between us growing ever smaller.

This is possible because by working through the traumatic memories in stages one through three, the amnesiac walls that separated us have fallen. We have already reached cooperation, co-awareness and co-consciousness and fusion is the next step in that process.

As the gaps between all the parts of me have grown smaller, I have been able to think as one person going in one direction without the chaos I have known all my life.

The Powerful Article That Redefined My Thoughts on Integration and Fusion

I read an article four years ago written by Rachel Downing, L.C.S.W.C. It had been posted on the Sidran Institute website and until recently I didn't understand what she was talking about.

In fact, the first time I read her piece, it disturbed me and made me angry.

Ms. Downing was polyfragmented and in her mid-40s when she began the final stage of fusion. She feared that she was too old, and she had too many alters to fuse, yet her therapist reassured her she was not.

For those of you who are new to DID lingo, polyfragmented means there are hundreds of alters in the system. This comes about by many years of horrendous abuse and/or torture.

Ms. Downing was speaking of one of the fears I've had, and I've heard others express, that we are too old and polyfragmented to fuse and should just not try.

Another fear Rachel Downing expressed to her therapist was that she would find it too difficult, if not impossible, to remember memories of her past and successfully work through them without her alters.

Once again, her therapist intervened, reminding her that people who have not any alters are still able to successfully process trauma memories.

I remember thinking that the memories were trapped in my alters, so without them, I would be unable to remember let alone put them into the context of the past. I have, like Ms. Downing, found this is not true.

Upon remembering a number of memories through my alters, I eventually found I didn't need to become them to remember what I had been through as them. It was okay to not force alters to remember traumatic events for me, I could do it on my own and perceive them from an adult's point of view.

This new perception was powerful.

Making the Decision to Speak in the First-Person

I realize this section may seem to some to be nit-picking, but I cannot express how important referring to yourself in the first-person is to the healing process and fusion.

Like you, all my life I've thought and spoken of myself in the plural. This happened when I was alone and speaking to someone else. I would use the term "we" instead of "I", which earned me funny looks more than once.

However, speaking in the plural about myself is detrimental in that it invites the fragmentation and chaos to continue. So long as I could say "WE" instead of "ME" I could hide my thoughts, feelings, and emotions behind the veil of dissociation.

Remember, everything you have or will ever do isn't happening to someone else, they are all your thoughts and behaviors.

One person doing many different actions.

Don't believe me? Have someone film you while you are dissociated, and then watch the video. Yes, you may see a manifestation of an alter such as clothing or hairstyle but look again as someone without knowledge of DID would see you.

I guarantee you will only see one body, one face, one person, not many.

If they open your skull to do brain surgery, they will not see lots of different brains or people inside.

They will only see one brain.

So long as you keep using the plural "WE" when referring to yourself, you will perpetuate the myth that you are more than one person and keep yourself from healing as far as you can go from dissociative identity disorder.

The chaos will continue.

The Drawbacks of Refusing and the Power of Allowing Fusion

One of the greatest drawbacks from refusing to allow yourself to reach fusion is that you will continue to experience helplessness.

When you were a child you were indeed helpless, but now you are a grownup and the opposite is true. You and only you control your present and your future.

By not allowing yourself to reach and complete fusion, you rob yourself of the power that being all grown up brings into our lives.

We can choose where we want to live, who we want to love, where we want to work and get ourselves away from abusive, traumatic relationships.

By choosing not to finish integration, we leave ourselves vulnerable to and in control of those who harmed us as children. They, through our alters, will forever be in charge and we will never know the power comes from taking charge.

There is wonderful power in fusion that can never be realized in dissociation.

Then there is the benefit from fusion of knowing and accepting yourself with all your flaws and beauty. No matter who you are, as a human, you have flaws.

However, it is also true that all humans are beautiful, even the people society does not like very much.

The chorus of humanity is made up of many different faces, beliefs, and understandings, and we who have been diagnosed with DID are part of it.

When you fuse nothing is lost.

The talents, knowledge, emotions, feelings, memories, and flaws that once were held in compartments called alters, after fusion become who you are in totality.

There is pride and power in fusion.

You Cannot Rush the Fourth Stage of Integration

Fusion occurs spontaneously.

You cannot rush into it, you can't even understand it very well until you reach it and only after going through the other three stages. I know this for a fact because until I was almost through the third stage, fusion made absolutely no sense.

I wish I could say that fusion is a quick process, but it is not. Depending on your therapist, temperament, and fragmentation fusion can take a few years or decades.

But, you know what? That's okay.

The healing journey is challenging and sometimes fraught with danger, but the self-awareness and self-respect you gain along the way are priceless.

It has taken me three decades to reach fusion, but I didn't have someone like me explaining the process and the pitfalls of healing. I had nothing to go on (and neither did my therapist) to help me along my healing journey, so I got stuck many times along the way.

That's the main reason I share my travels and what I have found with you on this website, to try and help you not fall into the same traps I have.

The important thing to always remember is that even though you might not fuse your last alter until you are on your deathbed, the process of healing will have taught you much about yourself and others.

I have a much deeper understanding about life and the world than most anyone I know. This awareness is directly attributable to working on the issues that caused me to not fuse into one during my early childhood.

The process of integration to reach fusion is a process that leads to much self-love and self-appreciation.

Choosing Fusion is Powerful but Takes Maintenance

Multiplicity is a way of life, and we sometimes get stuck in it because we feel that we will have no specialness or identity without it. What I've been trying to share here is that multiplicity is a cage and to escape the prisons we have forged for ourselves as adults, we must make some decisions.

The decisions we make are hard, there can be no doubt about that, and we will make many mistakes along the way. However, if we do not make those decisions, such as to allow ourselves to experience fusion, we are cheating ourselves just and maybe more as the people who harmed us when we were kids.

Fusion can be but most likely will not be perfect nor permanent.

I'll be honest here and say that I am speculating on the permanence of fusion because I have not been in this stage very long and have not finished yet.

However, Rachel Downing speaks about the permanence of fusion in her article. She speaks of how she must remain keeping herself on guard for triggering situations and be aware of her emotions to keep herself from using her old standby coping mechanism of dissociation.

As I have begun fusion, I too have noted that I must remain on the alert so that I can handle triggering events as a whole person rather than a fragment. I also must keep myself away from extremely stressful situations that are unnecessary and make sure I get enough rest.

These are only a few of the things that I have found to be vital in the maintaining of my fusion.

In Conclusion

I realize that integration is a hard concept to swallow, and the fear that keeps many from finishing it. However, there really is no choosing integration as the first time you walk into your therapist's door for treatment, integration began.

Fusion is the final step in the integration process that DOES NOT mean anyone in your system will die or disappear. Rather, fusion means they become so close to you that their thoughts intermingle with yours and you think as one whole person.

I put it to you, that thinking, acting and being one person instead of many is who we were meant to be and that by fusing our alters we are putting the final nail in the coffin of those who harmed us so long ago.

"If you don't like something change it; if you can't change it, change the way you think about it." ~ Mary Engelbreit

The Mistake of Rushing Integration

I have been involved with a discussion with several people on Twitter and other places about healing from DID. During my interactions, it was pointed out to me that many people living with the disorder try to rush their healing.

While I fully understand, (boy do I), that we all want to get well "NOW!", healing from the effects of childhood trauma that causes DID is not a short process nor should it be rushed.

This article is my attempt to caution those who are healing to take their time and offer a glimpse of what the result will be if you take my advice.

The Misunderstandings of Mental Health Professionals that Lead to Mistakes

Training for mental health professionals about dissociative identity disorder is brief at best and sometimes doesn't exist at all. In fact, if a wannabe psychiatrist or therapist wants to understand DID, they will need to seek out special training.

This lack of training leaves mental health professionals grasping for straws and guessing at how to help clients who enter their offices needing their help.

Then there is the stigma among some of the mental health professional community that says that DID does not exist and should be treated as another diagnosis altogether. This leaves therapists in danger of being labeled as a believer in UFOs rather than serious mental health professionals serving the best interests of their clients.

The result of all the above is that any therapist not only must rely on what they read in books but causes them to not ask questions for fear of attracting negative attention to their practices.

I believe that is why there is such a misunderstanding among the mental health community on not only the proper treatment of dissociative identity disorder but also in how long healing takes. Because all they must go on is previous experience treating other clients for other disorders, many professionals think that healing from DID and reaching fusion should take only a year or two tops.

The Misunderstandings of Multiples that Lead to Mistakes

As I wrote in my last article, there are two misunderstandings among those in the DID community. One, that healing (integration) means becoming a "singleton" (someone who never formed DID), and two, that during healing alters will be destroyed.

These two misunderstandings, along with not accepting that healing will take many years or hard work hold people back from the personal power to be gained through integration.

Since I have spoken about this extensively in my previous post, I hope you will check it out here.

I have identified four stages of healing that I have gone through to get to where I am now. No, I am not perfectly healed and no, I have not stopped losing time totally. The fact is that I am forever a multiple, but that does not mean I have to live in the chaos and uncertainty I used to. That's why I have incorporated the information I have below into this piece.

The Four Stages of Integration (Healing from Dissociative Identity Disorder)

I offer as my qualifications of writing the following material the fact that I am a member of the DID community having been diagnosed in 1990 with dissociative identity disorder. I have been on my healing journey since then, and to be honest have almost died on my travels. I speak as one who has conquered many barriers and reached fusion, the final stage of integration.

I do not hold anything higher than an associate degree in psychology and am not a mental health professional. I only have my lived experiences with my own healing to offer and ask only that I am heard, and that you consider what I have to say.

A Brief Discussion of Integration

Dissociative identity disorder (DID) is a coping mechanism that kept us alive and sane during severely traumatic childhoods. It cannot and will not heal overnight.

Healing takes many years of hard and sometimes dangerous mental work. It is a mistake to presume that it will only take a year of visits to a therapist to "fix" the problem. One cannot heal from a traumatic childhood, and you should not try.

Integration is a word describing the process of reaching the point where the chaos of dissociation ends. It does not mean any parts die, nor does it mean a person living with DID (multiple) becomes someone who does not (singleton).

Rather, integration means the alters of your internal system understanding one another, reaching cooperation and co-consciousness and thinking plus acting as one person.

Why So Many Multiples Fail to Integrate

As with the five stages of grief, integration does not happen in a linear fashion. One tends to bounce back and forth among the stages of healing and in and out of denial.

A lack of understanding of the definition of the integration process by multiples and mental health professionals plus trying to rush healing are the main culprits when people give up and decide to live the way they always have.

However, if a multiple decides to remain completely splintered, then they miss out on the power to their control life and be responsible for it. They miss out on what it is like to pool all the knowledge, talents and courage of who you are into one strong person that can make life goals and reach them.

I fully acknowledge that every multiple system has the right to choose to integrate or not, but I strongly encourage everyone to at least consider what I have said.

The Four Stages

Stage 1 Diagnosis: Stage one involves discovering that there is a name for what you have been experiencing all your life. Suddenly, all the strange things that have been happening in your adult life, the disappearance and reappearance of money, clothes, etc., make sense.

This can be one of the hardest and most denial-filled stages to the recovery of someone diagnosed with dissociative identity disorder. It is almost more traumatic than the events that caused the disorder because one is thrust into understanding what happened to cause you to form DID and the shock of knowing, finally, what has been going on.

Usually, it is in stage one that many seek out a therapist to help them heal. From the moment you walk into your first therapy appointment, you have begun the process of integration.

During stage one, multiples are becoming aware of what happened to them in childhood and these memories can make us feel dirty, unwanted and alone. Sometimes the memories held by the alters come forcefully to the surface in the form of flashbacks and panic attacks that hit us from nowhere and from triggers we do not yet understand.

Because of these intrusive thoughts and feelings, chaos ensues as we try our best to conquer the emotions of worthlessness and hopeless coming to us from our past. Grieving over what should have been comes into play during this stage as we become aware that our childhoods were marked with horrendous trauma and neglect. We grieve for the childhoods that were stolen from us.

Stage 2 Acceptance: Acceptance is a hard-earned step in healing from DID. It is here that we have accepted what happened to us as our history and that it is unalterable. There is no way to return to the past and rewrite it, at least not in reality although it can be done mentally.

The chaos of the first stage still happens, but for a different reason. As we learn the names and memories of the alters, we are met with resistance from them. Some feel threatened because they are afraid we cannot handle their thoughts, and others want desperately to be rescued.

Switching may become more prominent during this phase, and it is important to establish some way for all in the multiple system to communicate. This is the very beginnings of becoming co-aware and co-conscious.

It is here that we also, like every other human being, the culmination of our experiences. We are who we are because of the trauma we endured. We are strong, resilient, and wonderful people who have survived the un-survivable.

During the acceptance stage, we learn how to cope with what we have remembered about our history and begin to put them into proper context. This does not mean we minimize them, but rather that we acknowledge they happened. We learn that our alters saved our lives plus our sanity and begin to have a sense of respect for them.

Stage 3 Cooperation: Stage three is a vital one for it is here that we learn to bring our inner parts closer together than ever before because most of the amnesiac barriers come down. The walls come down because when all the members of our system know about each other due to being introduced to one another.

The safe place that you made in your mind so that communication becomes possible between the alters is vital to this stage. Sitting about together and laying down ground rules for the behavior of the alters in your system must happen first. The chaos of someone taking over and hurting the entire system financially or otherwise needs to be addressed and solutions found for times when an alter might feel triggered to life.

It is also during these discussions among the alters that cooperation begins. Everyone should have a say in your goals and hopes.

During stage three, an amazing thing begins to take place. You find that the fear and distrust you and your system had for each other has eased and has been replaced with love.

Eventually, the days when of chaos disappear and with a few exceptions so does the switching. You have become co-aware and co-conscious of each other's feelings, thoughts and this brings the self-discovery of all the skills learned during your lifetime.

Stage 4 Fusion: Stage four is hard to describe and many people living with dissociative identity disorder fear this one most of all.

Many are afraid that fusion means the disappearance of the alters or pushing them away into oblivion. This is absolutely not true. You can not destroy or rid yourself of alters because they are ALL parts of you. If they die you do and vice versa. No one is going anywhere.

Fusion means accepting the alters in your system as parts of you, but you beginning to think, speak and act as one person instead of many. You incorporate all these wonderful parts of yourself and their abilities into the strong and vital person you were

meant to be. You take full responsibility for your actions
whether you experience dissociation or not.

Fusion is not becoming a singleton. That is impossible. During
early childhood (usually agreed the age of 5) there is a stage
when the personality of children coalesce was missed by people
living with dissociative identity disorder. Our brains have been
altered in structure and cannot re-enter the missed
developmental stage.

We are forever changed.

However, we can learn to think and act as singletons with the
understanding that we are not and realize that with enough stress
we will fall back on our old coping mechanism, switching.

While the process of integration isn't a perfect one, it is much
better than living in the chaos of switching from alter to alter.

The Orchestra Illustration of Integration

I wrote the orchestra illustration several years ago and have
tweaked it as I have begun to understand my own road to
healing. I did so to help people understand better what I mean by
integration is a process that is an important part of healing.
While I understand and agree that every multiple system has the
right to choose to integrate or not, I strongly encourage you to
do so. To not reach fusion, the final stage in the integration
process is to deny yourself reaching a state where you have the
power that is present in all the alters in your system hold.

I have NOT always known this stuff, rather it came through
spending a lot of time and tears while I traveled down the road
less taken.

You can read the orchestra illustration earlier in this book.

Pulling it All Together

Too often multiples and their therapists try to move on from one stage of healing to another too quickly. Feeding off the lack of training of many professionals and the "I want healing NOW!" feelings of their clients, many mistakes are made leaving multiples feeling frustrated.

Not only are multiples frustrated, but because they rushed into healing and were not able to successfully reach fusion, they give up on the whole idea.

Let me tell you for a moment how I am today as compared to many years ago.

My therapist, Paula, had no training in dealing with DID so I was an enigma for her that challenged her abilities as a therapist. As I have stated, I was diagnosed in 1990, before people had PC's and laptops in their homes to do research. That meant Paula had to rely on what she could find at the library and her instincts to guide her.

We made many mistakes in attempting my healing. The first and perhaps the one that held me back the most was that neither of us knew how to approach integration. Paula tried to help me age the alters from children to adulthood, but I now know that was a mistake. I hadn't remembered all I needed to from them and they weren't aware enough of one another to accomplish fusing the littles together.

The other mistake was created by me. I found it very difficult to tell Paula everything she needed to know to understand where I was in my healing. For one, I neglected to tell her that helping the littles to be adults was not just failing but was proving impossible. I also failed to allow her to see my emotions and to speak to the other alters. It was like we were playing a game and were terrified of her disappearing on us.

Only after I lost Paula to a bankruptcy, spent seven and a half years inpatient on a psychiatric ward, and was miraculously able to return to her office that I had learned the value of being honest with Paula.

By the time I was in Paula's office again, I had spent plenty of time thinking about our mistakes in my treatment and because I refused to play games healing sped up enormously.

Paula retired in 2015 leaving me grieving her loss but I have continued to travel down the road to healing without her.

Late last year, I came to three understandings that have been vital to where I am today.

One, you cannot see stage 3 from 1. This is true of all the stages. You CAN look back, but visualizing, understanding and accepting future stages is impossible. That's why when I speak of stage four, fusion, so many people resist even the thought of doing it.

Two, fusion happens when you understand that it is much better to see yourself as a cohesive "I" than a splintered "WE." I know that will meet with resistance from many, but the power of living life thinking as a "ME" is powerful.

Three, giving up the identity of a multiple is very tough. Paula, throughout the years we spent together, constantly challenged me by asking me what I would lose if I didn't identify as a multiple anymore. When I approached fusion, I finally had the answer to her probing questions. Somehow, I felt I would be less special and less unique.

Now I have discovered, strangely enough, that just the opposite has happened. I find myself in a minority of people who have been diagnosed with dissociative identity disorder who have reached fusion. Sigh. One never knows.

Fusion has brought enormous power to my life. I still have alters, but they are so close that we tend to think as one. I can't express how much quieter and happier I am since losing time and switching have become rare. I am powerful and ready to conquer just about anything.

Watch out world!

I hope this article has helped in some small way. Shirley

"Trauma is personal. It does not disappear if it is not validated.
When it is ignored or invalidated the silent screams continue
internally heard only by the one held captive. When someone
enters the pain and hears the screams healing can begin." ~
Danielle Bernock, *Emerging with Wings: A True Story of Lies,
Pain, and the Love That Heals*

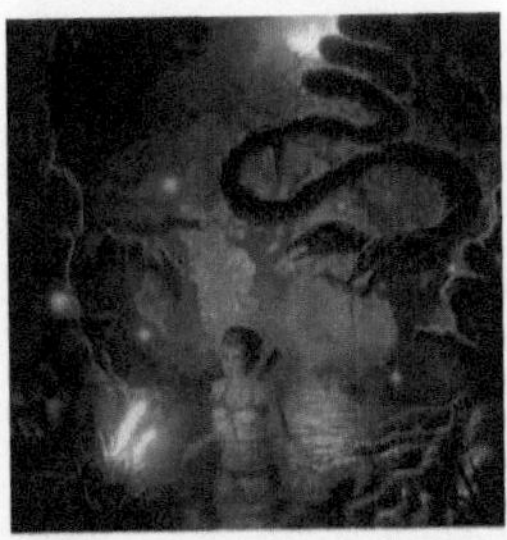

When Fantasy is Your Friend

Growing up in an abusive home, children often find they have nowhere to go and no place to turn. So, they turn to their imaginations to help them cope.

I'm writing this post out of my own experiences with the pretend world I lived in as a kid. I'll try not to be triggering, but the sadness I feel when discussing this topic may show through.

Life in Hell

Living in my house was like living in a war zone. One never knew when a bomb shell would explode nearby and make you a causality. There was constant yelling, bickering, and other unpleasant noise and abuse that I was only too eager to escape.

Before age nine I would spend my time outdoors playing as hard as I could. I wanted desperately to be part of a family that ate regular meals, had a clean house and like each other. That was not my reality.

When the weather was too foul to play outside, before the advent of cable television, I resorted to make believe and books to cope. I had a set of Happy Hollister books and read all of them twice. This was at the age of six. By the time I was eight I had read all our encyclopedias. It was much simpler to block out the noise and pretend I wasn't there if I had my head in a book. I could pretend I was in faraway places living with animals or exploring strange worlds.

After age nine, I decided not to play outside anymore. We had moved to Illinois from Tennessee and I was in shock. Compared to the modern conditions of being and living near a Naval base that I had been raised in, Illinois was old and very different. I spoke with a strong southern accent and the other kids wasted no time making fun of me. To make matters worse, some of the neighborhood kids were sexually confused and abusive. To me it was horrifying to realize that I was no safer outside than in. So, I stopped going out.

I began to spend hours upon hours closed-up in my bedroom. I still had books and got interested in listening to music. For my ninth birthday my father bought me a little transistor radio with an earphone and I would listen to it constantly. When I could pull myself out of my room, I'd watch hour upon hour of television. I wanted my family to be like the ones I saw every day in television reruns. They loved and supported each other and didn't yell. Then they would solve whatever problem was perplexing them in under an hour.

As a teenager I preferred the safety of my bedroom to the unexpected that I could expect among my peers. I went on zero dates during my teenage years hiding inside books and trying desperately to be invisible. The abuse I suffered at the hands of a man in my family became overwhelming during these turbulent developmental years, and after I told on him and was subsequently disowned by that side if the family, my despair grew ever deeper. I think the only thing that kept me from dying by suicide at that tender age was my being a multiple.

To this day, I'm not certain if that was good or bad. Had I died then I think it would have been better.

Fantasy was my only escape from a world that did not want me and from my own emotions connected with not being wanted.

Fantasy Was My Way of Coping

Tragically, I know while reading this many of you understand what I am saying and can relate. When living in hell, one tends to find ways to cope, and fantasy is a wonderful escape.

On top of this, we had already formed alters to help us. We were not alone when we isolated then nor are we now. I have been in my bedroom all day today isolating myself from my family. I feel safe if I'm cocooned in here with my door closed.

I feel horribly saddened that we had to go through what we did as kids. We should never have had to find solace in the fantasy of books, make believe and television. We needed and deserved so much better.

Today my brother and his wife have been having some problems, and I have been very triggered. I am fighting very hard to stay in the present. My heart and mind want to time travel back to the days when I was a kid and relive the horror of those days. I do not. Yes, my alters are all me and I them, but most of me does not wish to live in trauma-time any longer. I am very upset with the other two adults in my household who have such reckless regard for the emotional states of myself and my very young nephew.

Unlike my nephew, I do not bounce back quickly after hearing the yelling disturbance that went on this morning. Yes, I realize that married couples sometimes bicker, but they know how upset I become when I am forced to listen to such bullshit. Sigh.

 I guess I wanted to write this piece to say this.

I am not a know-it-all. I do not have the answers. I never claimed to. I am just an average Joe-Blow who survived things that should have killed me. Today I feel like giving up. I don't care if I live or die. Admitting that isn't easy for me because I am one of the people I wrote about in my previous article. I smile the entire time I am feeling dead inside.

Nope, no pep talk today. No smiling when I feel like shit. Just honesty so that I can in some way connect with you and say, "Hey, I'm just like you."

"Honesty and frankness make you vulnerable. Be honest and frank anyway." Kent M.

I admired her.

Not for her for her smile, though it was beautiful.

Not for her eyes, though they shone brightly.

I admired her.

For the little scars and war wounds

That she displayed proudly for the world to see

I admired her for her strength and her courage.

Poem by S. Marie

A Story of Friendship

I have had some people ask me recently what at first might seem an odd question. However, I am convinced it is very important.

What is friendship?

Some may giggle to think that someone wouldn't understand what a friendship is, but you won't when you are done with this article.

A definition I found on an online dictionary has this definition of friendship:

> "The emotions or conduct of friends, the state of being friends. Relationship. Attachment. Bond. Link. Union. Understanding. Harmony. A state of mutual trust and support."

So, what is your definition of friendship?

I'm not writing this piece because I have all the answers. I've had just one friend in my lifetime whom I can honestly say I trusted completely.

Her name was Barbara June York.

Barb and I were friends for 27 years. We had a lot in common in the first fifteen of those years. We were both people who were raised by alcoholics and both had childhood trauma histories.

Wow. How many of us have someone we feel all those things about who reciprocate 100%?

Today I am going to share the story of my best friend Barb. Ours was a unique friendship to be sure.

At one time we were closer than two peas in a pod. We helped each other through the hard times we both faced in therapy. She too had been a victim of childhood violence and we shared a great deal in common in other ways too.

So, here is the story of my forever friendship with Barbara June.

Barbara June

Friendship is something I've always found difficult. Not that I cannot be a good friend, but that I have a hard time trusting others and letting others share my world. Having survived severe childhood trauma, I struggled with getting close to anyone. Then one evening I met Barbara June.

I had begun going to a twelve-step program for those who love alcoholics, and one evening we had a new member. She was articulate and brave, but I could tell she was in trouble. I invited her to go to a local pizza parlor after the meeting and found I was right. She was feeling the need to die by suicide. After we talked for several hours we parted, and I was fearful she would not survive.

A few days later I received a phone call, it was Barbara June. She wanted to thank me for helping her that night in the pizza parlor and wanted to know if I would like to go shopping. I had no money, but I wanted to hang-out with Barb, so I said yes. It wasn't long before we became close friends and confidantes.

Barb lived in a **small-town** half an hour from my home. This was in a decade before the popularity of cell phones, and she had no phone. So, she would go on top of a dam that was located near her apartment and use the pay phone. She would dial my number and then close the phone receiver in with her in her car and we'd talk for hours.

We began hanging out with each other every weekend spending most of our time just driving out in the country. We lived in an area which harbored a large Amish population and loved looking at their horses and talking about their simple lifestyle. One afternoon we noticed a plume of smoke in the distance and decided to go and see if we could find out what was burning.

We drove along, looking up at the smoke to see where to turn next and found ourselves on a dirt road. Suddenly we came upon a scene that shook both of us to our core. A cornfield was on fire and was being whipped by the wind towards a large country home whose residents were fleeing as we drove up.

I was driving my old station wagon and it suddenly occurred to me that the flames were heading straight for us at a break-taking pace. I threw the car in reverse and whipped it around to rush away from the fire and we just managed to get away before it crossed the road to the house.

Barbara June and I had many adventures and cried many tears together in our twenty-seven-year friendship. We laughed and cried together as well as helped each other when we were depressed or afraid.

The first time I was admitted to an inpatient psychiatric ward Barb took me and stayed with me for a while. I was petrified to be there, and she sat with me holding me to help calm me down.

Barb was the only person outside my professional care, who ever met a child alter. They adored her and as did all the members of my system.

Like I said, we had many adventures together and it was me who suggested that she attend college to become a therapist. Barb graduated with her master's degree, sometime in the early 2000's. I say sometime because I was living inpatient in a psychiatric ward by then.

Barb rescued greyhounds and adopted three for herself. That's the kind of heart Barb had. She was kind and even though her dogs arrived terrified and shaking, they soon felt right at home in her care.

It was during the seven years when I was living inpatient that we became more distant from each other. Our friendship had radically changed when she became a therapist. I had to constantly remind her that she was my friend not my therapist because she began to analyze me instead of listening as a friend.

But our friendship survived, and we were still very close. Barbara June was like the big sister I never had. I left the long-term facility where I had lived for over seven years in 2011 and we began to hang out together again.

Then in October of 2013 Barb called to tell me she had Leukemia. I felt my heart sink in my chest knowing that the survival rate for adults, unlike children, is very low.

She entered a hospital in a distant city (Chicago) where I could not go and see her. I sent her a letter a day to give her encouragement. She fought for her life for many months and was finally allowed to return home in mid-2014.

Although I knew Barb was still very ill, she neglected to tell me that she had been sent home to die. The hospital knew they had done all they could to help her and gave her permission to return home because Barb insisted she needed to be with her beloved greyhounds and to sleep in her own bed.

In March 2015 just when the spring flowers were making their way out of the chilly soil, I received a phone call that to this day haunts me. My best friend had died in her sleep.

Barbara June was no more.

Barb's memorial service was held in early summer with only her close friends and co-workers in attendance. A violinist played lovely, lilting music as we spoke among ourselves of how much we had loved Barbara June and all the beauty she had brought to the world.

I didn't cry tears that day, in fact, I have not wept since her death. Barb lives on in my soul as the warm, caring and loving person that I knew and loved.

The world is a lot colder now that she has gone.

I loved Barbara June with all my heart and she will never be forgotten as long as I am alive.

Goodbye Barbara June.

Goodbye, my good friend.

Barbara June

I sit here today full of sorrow
I've lost you, my best friend
You and I were close as flower petals
We knew each other's hearts
We knew each other's fears
And we knew how to find strength in one another
One day you died and left me alone
So cold, so cold, so cold
The world is colder and harsher now
I know you had no choice to die
But that doesn't stop my grief
I miss you with all my soul
My best friend, my confidante
Barbara June

~Shirley J. Davis

The Neuroscience of Shame

In the previous post, we examined the different types of shame, but what happens in the brain to make shame benign or toxic? What parts of our brains are injured by chronically being shamed by our caregivers, and how does that change who we are?

These are a few of the questions I will attempt to answer in this piece. Some of the language regarding regions of the brain may be new to you, so I will give you a brief description of them, and links so you can research them yourself.

The Autonomic Nervous System (ANS) and Shame

The autonomic nervous system is the part of our nervous system that controls and regulates the internal organs without the need to think about it. There are two branches to the ANS, the sympathetic and parasympathetic nervous systems.

The sympathetic nervous system is responsible for connecting the different organs of our bodies to our brains through our spinal cord. When we perceive danger, our sympathetic nervous system causes us to prepare to fight/flight/or freeze by increasing our heart rate, increasing blood flow to our muscles, and decreasing blood flow to organs such as the skin.

The sympathetic nervous system, as we can see, is excitatory to the body.

The parasympathetic nervous system, is comprised of nerve fibers or cranial nerves. The primary part of the parasympathetic nervous system is the vagus nerve, and the lumbar spinal nerves.

Upon stimulation, these important structures increase digestive secretions and reduce the heartbeat.

The parasympathetic nervous system, as we can see, is calming to the body.

When faced with shame, the brain reacts as if it were facing a physical danger, and activates the sympathetic nervous system generating the flight/fight/freeze response.

The flight response triggers the feeling of needing to disappear, and children who have this occur will try to become invisible. They will literally look smaller and their expression become blank.

However, the fight response expresses itself as verbal and behavioral aggression by the embarrassed person towards the other who caused them to feel ashamed.

The freeze response is what normally occurs when people are faced with trauma where they feel trapped and powerless. The freeze response allows us to survive situations where intolerable things are happening to us.

The freeze response to shame has negative consequences too.

The freeze response upsets our ability to think clearly, and we decide that we are stuck in a situation where we have no power because we have something wrong with us.

It can cause us to believe that what is happening or has happened is our fault.

Clearly, in most cases, situations such as childhood trauma and adult rape are never our fault. We have become victims of violence.

Shame: What Infants Learns

From birth, we humans are hardwired to interact with our caregivers. We seek close connections with them to survive and to aid our brains to develop.

Soon after birth, we begin storing in our brains how our needs are met by our caregivers. These important interactions between our caregivers and ourselves are stored in our limbic system in a structure called the amygdala, allowing responses from our caregivers to be stored in implicit memory.

(I have described the limbic system, the amygdala and the hippocampus in other posts. Please follow the links for further information.)

Through the information we store in our brains about the responses of our caregivers, we develop anticipation of the trustworthiness of relationships based on our early experiences.

In short, we learn to interpret life through the lens of the messages we learn from our caregivers.

Shame is an emotion that can save children from injury or death by engraining into their brain an appropriate response to danger. A good example would be a child running into the street.

When children are yes "no" by a caregiver to stop them from running into the street, the sympathetic system (the excitatory response) is activated triggering the fight/flight/freeze response.

The child (hopefully) will freeze and then because their sympathetic nervous system is on high alert, they will begin to cry.

If the caregiver immediately goes to their child and gives them calming reassurance, the child's parasympathetic nervous system becomes activated and the child's arousal will subside.

The child in this scenario grows up with the propensity to follow what they were taught about danger and how to recognize it. When faced with a perceived danger, they will be able to draw on what they learned that day from their caregiver and respond appropriately.

Also, when they feel shame for doing something wrong to someone else, they immediately recognize their actions and do what they need to calm their triggered sympathetic nervous system response.

However, what if the caregiver uses toxic shame to control their child.

In this scenario, the caregiver says "no" often and does so to meet their own needs and not to help their child. To make matters worse, they never or rarely follow up their message with any calming reassurance.

In this case, when the child's sympathetic nervous system is triggered, they enter a state of arousal. They feel fear and freeze at first, and then begin to cry.

However, because there is no reassurance, the parasympathetic nervous system is not triggered and does not do its job of calming them down.

The Threat to Relational Bonds in Adulthood

A child exposed to toxic shame has a conundrum. Their brain experiences the arousal of the sympathetic nervous system and the acceleration of the parasympathetic nervous system at the same time.

The result, that like an automobile, they sit and spin their tires unable to move forward in their understanding of other relationships they encounter later in life. This is because the toxic shame experienced in childhood impacts the hippocampus, another part of the limbic system responsible for consolidating memory.

In childhood, our hippocampi have internalized into our memory how we should respond to situations where we feel uncomfortable or uncertain. If we were mistreated, our hippocampi internalize negative messages about ourselves and what we can expect from others.

The effect is that later in life, when we encounter uncomfortable situations that our hippocampi thinks is in any way similar to what we encountered in childhood, we feel shame.

This triggered response then sends us spiraling into a complicated dance of arousal and fear that adversely affects how we form new relationships with others.

The late Dr. John Bradshaw, in his book, *Healing the Shame that Binds You* stated the following:

"Prolonged shame states early in life can result in permanently dysregulated autonomic functioning and a heightened sense of vulnerability to others. Their lives are marked by a chronic anxiety, exhaustion, depression and a losing struggle to achieve perfection."

The Important Work of the Insula

Toxic shame, a term first coined by Sylvan Tomkins in the early 1960s, can cause many mental health issues because it generates the formation of a low self-esteem, anxiety, irrational guilt, perfectionism and addiction.

However, recent research using functional magnetic resonance imaging (fMRI) studies tell an even larger story.

In a paper published in the journal *Social Cognition Affective Neuroscience* in 2014, researchers carried out fMRI studies on subjects to determine if and where the brain reacts to shame.

The researchers followed an imaging paradigm originally employed by Takahashi et. al. that the research team adapted from Japanese culture to their German culture.

Their researchers showed shame inducing stimuli to test subjects as they lay in an fMRI machine to see where in the brain they saw activation by measuring blood flow.

What they observed changed the way we look at the brain and its response to shame.

The research team found several vital brain regions reacted to shame stimuli, including the frontal lobe which contains both the amygdala and a little known (at that time) brain structure called the insula.

The insula was once believed to be a brain structure that was implicated in emotional responses and part of the limbic system.

However, the findings in yet another study conducted at the University of Melbourne in Australia in 2014, has shed new light on this formerly misclassified structure.

The insula is now believed to be involved in awareness (consciousness) and play an important role in other functions believed linked to emotion including self-awareness and interpersonal experiences.

In fact, research has given new insight into the critical role the insula plays as it is the hub that regulates the interactions between brain regions that regulate our internal focus of our bodies and how we regulate our behavior.

When confronted by an unusual and outstanding event, the insula functions to mark the event for further processing and then initiates the appropriate brain region's response to it.

Impact of Trauma on the Insula

In a previous series on the effects of childhood trauma, I wrote a post where we examined how childhood trauma changes the developing brain. We saw how trauma causes many portions of a child's brain to not mature correctly and how this immaturity brings dysfunction and emotional problems later in life.

A study reported in Neuroscience News speaks on a research team's findings of the developmental changes in the insula of people who had developed complex post-traumatic stress disorder (CPTSD) in childhood.

To refresh your minds, CPTSD develops when children are exposed to traumatic stress, such as child abuse, living in a war zone, or chronic physical illnesses. People living with CPTSD may experience flashbacks, avoidance behaviors, social isolation, and difficulty with sleeping and concentrating.

The study I mentioned above was performed using MRI scans of the brains of 59 children between the ages of 9-17. Thirty of the children, 14 girls and 16 boys, had symptoms of trauma and 29 other children, 15 girls and 14 boys, had no symptoms of having lived through trauma. These latter children served as the control group for the study.

The researchers saw no differences in the brain structures of the boys and girls in the non-traumatized control group, but what they saw in the group of traumatized children shocked them.

The insula structure of the brains of the boys in the traumatized group had larger volumes and surface areas than the control group and were dramatically smaller in the brains of the girls.

Their study highlighted two new important new findings.

One, trauma not only impacts the insula of the developing brains of children, it also impacts boys and girls differently.

Two, since insula value decreases with aging (Shaw et. al., 2008), the reduction of insula volumes in girls with CPTSD suggests that their insula is prematurely aging due to traumatic stress.

Since the insula is known to be associated with the emotions of disgust and shame, one can see why so many women who have survived childhood trauma grow up to have such devastating mental health issues as anorexia nervosa, bulimia and other eating disorders.

Pulling it All Together

I realize that this article has been highly technical and full of unfamiliar terminology. However, there is one important message I want you to take away from reading it.

That message is this; you are neither weird because of the emotional problems you may be experiencing from childhood trauma, nor are you without hope.

Although your brain has sustained developmental damage from what happened to you as a kid, that does not mean those problems cannot be rectified.

Thanks to **neuroplasticity**, your brain can learn and adapt to new ways of thinking and behaving. There is a myriad of different ways to accomplish these brain changes, and our next article will focus on the different types of treatment options available to help you overcome the traumatic events that harmed your brains development.

Depression, eating disorders such as bulimia and anorexia nervosa, Post-Traumatic Stress Disorder and Complex Post-Traumatic Stress Disorder are only a few of the mental health issues related to toxic shame.

The messages we internalized in childhood or as adults during a highly traumatic event, both cause feelings helplessness and victimization. We see life and other human beings as potential threats to our well-being and our limbic systems are constantly on the alert in a hyper-aroused state looking for danger.

The damage to our self-esteem limits our ability to seek out and enjoy satisfying relationships and may keep us from achieving professional success. We may be consumed with self-hate, rage and feel alienated from the people around us.

In short, we are terrified. We are afraid to trust someone else because they might hurt us. We are afraid to reach for a better job or to seek out a meaningful profession because we might fail. We isolate ourselves in a cocoon of anxiety and guilt.

Some of us will become codependent on others because we feel we must care for others and that taking care of ourselves is wrong. We may be afraid that once we have found someone, we must maintain that relationship at all costs because we will never find anyone else. We think to ourselves, "No one else will ever want me."

The isolation, fear, or codependency leaves us trapped in a
quagmire of pain that we need help to escape.

The Mind in State

Does consciousness exist only when
you name it? Was the double helix a
stranger, the nucleus the first brain?

I feel therefore I am.

This is more
peptide than pep-talk.

The tongue-less
mood is sticking its tongue out at us.
The mountain wool is shaved into
vineyards.

Without other there is no
self & and we are not always other of
other selves.

Is the moon a self, is
wine or grape?

The body & the as-if
body, taking time taste waking slow
rain healing grass.

~ Fady Joudah

Psychotherapy

One of the most important treatments for the effects of complex trauma for adults is psychotherapy. Sitting with another adult who is trained in the listening profession is a powerful method to exchange the old tapes that were installed by our traumatic experiences.

In this first article, we are going to explore together the types of psychotherapy and Therapists, and the different methods they employ to help their clients overcome the side-effects of complex trauma.

What is Psychotherapy?

An article written by Michael Herkov, Ph.D. for the website Psych Central offers the following very good definition of psychotherapy:

"Psychotherapy -- also called "talk therapy" or just plain therapy -- is a process whereby psychological problems are treated through communication and relationship factors between an individual and a trained mental health professional. Modern psychotherapy is time-limited, focused, and usually occurs once a week for 45-50 minutes per session."

For some of you who have never experienced psychotherapy, the term may conjure in your mind images of someone lying on a couch while their therapist sits with pen and paper in hand jotting down what you are saying.

However, while it is true that therapists pay close attention to your words, they are normally facing you and you are both sitting in comfortable chairs. They may have a pen and some paper handy, but usually they take mental notes of what they feel the important aspects of your session.

The therapist will not only be aware of your words, they will also be actively watching your body language because we often say more with our bodies than with our mouth.

The Different Types of Therapists

Therapists, like many professions, has different types of training and thus different types of therapists. It is important to be aware of this because what you need in a therapist may vary widely and you will need to make an informed choice when looking for a counselor.

The National Alliance on Mental Health (NAMI) offers this breakdown of the different types of therapists.

Psychologists. Psychologists hold a doctoral degree in clinical psychology or another specialty such as counseling or education. They are trained to evaluate a person's mental health using clinical interviews, psychological evaluations and testing. They can make diagnoses and provide individual and group therapy. Some may have training in specific forms of therapy like cognitive behavioral therapy (CBT), dialectical behavior therapy (DBT) and other behavioral therapy interventions (we'll discuss these different types of therapy treatments in another post).

A Psychologist has earned an advanced college degree of either a Doctor of Philosophy (Ph.D.) or in a field of psychology such as research or forensics (Phys. D.).

Counselors, Clinicians, and Therapists. These masters-level health care professionals are trained to evaluate a person's mental health and use therapeutic techniques based on specific training programs. They operate under a variety of job titles—including counselor, clinician, therapist or something else—based on the treatment setting. Working with one of these mental health professionals can lead not only to symptom reduction but to better ways of thinking, feeling and living.

Counselors, Clinicians, and Therapists have earned a master's degree (M.S. or M.A.) in a mental health related field such as psychology or family therapy.

Clinical Social Workers. Clinical social workers are trained to evaluate a person's mental health and use therapeutic techniques based on specific training programs. They are also trained in case management and advocacy services.

A clinical social worker has earned a master's degree in social work (MSW), licensed independent social worker (LICSW), or licensed clinical social worker (LICSW).

A Trauma-Informed Therapist. A trauma-informed
therapist is aware of the complex impact of trauma (any
perceived trauma) on a person's suffering and how it shapes a
person's efforts to cope.

It also means that any person or organization that claims to
be trauma-informed makes emotional and psychological safety a
priority for the people they serve.

Trauma-informed therapists are any of the above licensed
professionals and may also include Psychiatrists and medical
professionals.

Reasons to Seek a Psychotherapist

The reasons people seek the assistance of a psychotherapist are
many and varied. Some look for help in the efforts to stop
smoking or lose weight. However, in the case of people who are
experiencing the lasting effects of complex trauma, utilizing the
skills of a psychotherapist is a must.

The reason I say that one needs to seek a therapist to overcome
the effects of complex trauma is that it can cause an enormous
number of cognitive (thinking) and emotional problems. We
know this because of a study conducted in the years 1995-1997
by Dr. Vincent Felitti, chief of Kaiser Permanente's Department
of Preventative Medicine.

(We have an extensive discussion of the ACE's study here.)

These problems include:

- Substance Abuse
- Depression
- Suicidality
- Borderline Personality Disorder
- Dissociative Disorders
- Anxiety disorders
- Depression
- Feelings of worthlessness and hopelessness
- Memory difficulties
- Troubles regulating emotion

- Problems concentrating
- Avoidance symptoms (subconscious fear that causes avoidance of places or people)
- Flashbacks
- Insomnia

It should be obvious that when one experiences the problems caused by complex traumatic experiences, our lives are difficult and chaotic.

When our lives have become too overwhelming and we feel lost, psychotherapy can help us regain our sense of control.

Why Does Therapy Work?

To be honest, although there are many theories as to why therapy works, no one really knows.

However, the best theory I found on when researching for this article was by a psychoanalyst Wilfred Bion who wrote "When two personalities meet, an emotional storm is created."

What did Dr. Bion mean by an emotional storm?

I think there are two explanations. The first is highlighted by Vanessa Bright, a Psychoanalyst in private practice. She states in her blog post Painfully Human that she believes what Dr. Bion meant by the term "emotional storm."

"Being human is difficult almost by definition and is why we find so many ways to avoid each other's emotional reality.

And I don't think I am alone in the recognition that despite the vulnerability it requires, being human together is much more healing than life in isolation through superficiality.

It takes practice, it takes work getting used to our "storms" (which may be a nanosecond or years), it takes work releasing that demand for perfection, and it takes work to just recognize that all of this is utterly, painfully human."

However, having experienced extensive psychotherapy for many years to heal from my own adverse childhood and highly traumatic experiences, I believe I have a better answer and it includes a reason why therapy works.

As Vanessa Bright suggest, we are all painfully human and sharing our experiences in life has a powerful impact on our healing from complex trauma.

It is my belief that the "emotional storm" that happens when a client and a therapist meet is a two-way street in sharing some of the most intimate moments anyone can share with another human being. The client brings their experiences and hurt to the therapist who in turn brings into the alliance their training but also their own lifetime events.

The emotional storm is the tornadic activity that goes on when the two very different experience and expectations of the therapist and client alliance come together.

The Importance of the Therapeutic Alliance

In war or peace time, an alliance between two or more countries secures a balance of power and aids in the defense from hostile countries. They form an understanding and often sign treaties established on common goals.

The therapeutic alliance is not much different.

In therapy, a vital process where a client and a therapist work together to defeat a common enemy, the lasting effects of complex trauma. Psychotherapy is a turbulent and dynamic relationship between the two parties, it is not a sterile non-caring environment for either the client or the therapist.

Research has found that a good therapeutic alliance can result in healing that lasts far beyond the original therapeutic experience.

Just like the rest of us, therapists are human beings and as such they bring to the table of the alliance with their clients not only their training but also their home lives and past experiences. Therapists are not superheroes, mind-readers or magicians.

Psychotherapy requires an enormous amount of courage, vulnerability and trust for it to work well and the therapeutic alliance allows all these things to develop over the course of treatment.

So, the therapeutic alliance is more than just learned knowledge on the part of the therapist from their training, it is a bond formed between client and therapist.

With that having been said, it is important to note that the therapeutic relationship is much different than any other type of relationships.

Your therapist is not your friend. That means that unlike other relationships in your life, your therapist will not share intimate details of her life with you and will not give you advice or tell you what to do. Neither will a therapist share the information you have shared with them with anyone else without your permission.

(Important Note: If you are danger to yourself or others, this rule does not apply.)

By not divulging personal information, a therapist is trying to be coy or secretive. Instead, the reason therapists do not divulge their personal information is simple. Your therapy should be centered around you, your goals, and your needs. By not divulging their personal information you are free to explore your own journey without being affected by obsessions with the life of your therapist.

A therapist will not give you advice nor tell you what to do. This means that he or she is not directly responsible for your choices nor living with the consequences of them. You are and always will be.

During your therapy, they may make suggestions for you to consider, but it is totally up to you to decide if you want to pursue those suggestions.

Your therapist will use questions to help guide you through the maze of emotions and memories to help you decide what you will do and how you will heal from them.

He or you will use reflective listening to "reflect" to you what you say to them. They do this for three reasons. One, to make certain they heard you correctly, two, to validate to you they are listening, and three, to allow you to hear your own words so you can examine them better.

The exception to this rule is, like the therapeutic alliance, is if they are concerned for you or someone else's safety. In this case, your therapist will make direct and overt directives with you.

The Boundaries of Psychotherapy

There are rules of engagement in any alliance, and a therapeutic alliance is no different. These rules are known as boundaries and they set the structure for the relationship to set both the client and therapist in a consistent, reliable and predictable path.

Your therapist has boundaries that they expect you to honor and remember. These rules ensure that both of you remain physically and emotionally safe during in the therapeutic alliance.

One very important boundary is that there will be no unwanted physical contact. Your therapist is bound by ethical rules not to hug, kiss or otherwise have physical contact with you.

This does not mean that if by mutual consent, you hug one another at the end of a session, but it does mean it is unethical for them to have any overt or other sexual contact with you.

There is a vital reason for strict ethical boundaries.

The power that a therapist can have over a client is considerable and using that power to exploit or use a client is horrendously wrong. For this reason, a therapist will express to you the limits of their contact with you.

There are other more benign boundaries such as your therapist telling you what form of communications they will accept between you. Some therapists allow their clients to email them and others don't. Some will allow you to call their homes if you are in crisis, others will not.

Therapy shouldn't take place in other venues other than the therapist's office. The reasons for this boundary is to protect the therapist and you. Holding a therapy session in a coffee shop threatens your right to privacy and going to your home for a session exposes a therapist to possible lawsuits involving unwanted sexual contact.

Your therapist will not allow themselves to become involved with you in secondary relationships. They are not your friend, they are your therapist. So, do not expect your therapist to attend a wedding, party or even to acknowledge you in public at all (unless you instigate the greeting) because of their concern to maintain the therapeutic alliance even outside the office.

Establishing and maintaining healthy boundaries between themselves and you, their client, helps them not experience emotional burn out. You can only imagine what a day in the life of a therapist must be like as they sit for hours listening to the problems and traumas of their clients.

Remember, always remember, they are human beings with emotions and feelings just like you. For this reason, they may take an unexpected day off when they cancel your appointment or take a week or two off for a vacation. They need time to decompress and take care of their and their family's needs. By establishing ground rules with you they are making sure they continue to be in a position where they can help you on your healing journey.

Concluding Our Time Together

Every therapist is different in their personality, approach and how they interact with their clients. They should from the very beginning your therapist will begin to form the therapeutic alliance with you. While they are doing this, they will establish the ground rules of what is expected from the two of you on the healing journey you will be taking together.

Getting to know each other and what to expect and not to expect from psychotherapy takes time. For some of us it takes more time than average.

I will give you a brief rundown of my own experience in psychotherapy.

I entered therapy in 1989 with a wonderful therapist named Paula. From the beginning I believe Paula knew our journey was going to be very long, dangerous and complicated.

For one, I had severe trust issues. I couldn't trust her at first at all and even after several years hid things from her. That's how damaging my childhood trauma had been.

Eventually, Paula became a mother figure to me. This made things difficult for her because while it was important to build my trust in her, to remain effective as a therapist she had to maintain her distance.

We worked on my issues for 14 years in total, and in all that time I never encroached upon or crossed the boundaries she had set for our alliance.

She had told me she would accept phone calls at her home if I were in crisis, but she would return my calls from her office.

She made it clear from the beginning that unless I asked for a hug, one would not be forthcoming.

She also explained to me that our therapy sessions together were my hour. If I wished to waste that hour discussing the weather or dissociating out of the room, she would chit chat or wait for me to return. There would be no extra time allotted for such things.

Paula retired in 2016, and at the conclusion of our time together, we left each other feeling as though we had accomplished the goals we had set together on my first time in her office.

I had my dignity and personal power intact and she felt a deep sense of accomplishment in that she had helped me heal.

Although I may never see Paula again, she will forever remain in my heart as the mother I never had. I can't help but believe that I have made an indelible mark on her heart as well.

Overcoming Shame to Live a New Life

Shame is the most powerful, master emotion. It's the fear that we're not good enough. ~ Brene' Brown

In this piece, we are going to explore the different ways that we can overcome shame to become who were always meant to be before shame drove us into our self-imposed cages.

Shame is Only Toxic When It Runs Your Life

As we discussed in a previous post, shame is a fundamental emotion that is necessary for us to understand our relationships to others. Without shame, we would have a tough time knowing what is and is not appropriate to say and do in our dealings with the people with whom we have relations. Shame keeps our tendencies to want to run other's lives in check and allows us to know when we need to apologize for something we have said or done.

However, if we grow up in homes where we are made to feel inadequate or have problems with other children where we are bullied, shame becomes a prison where we can get lost.

The term toxic shame was first coined by John Bradshaw in 1990 to describe the person whose thoughts, feelings and behaviors of who grew up in homes where they were repeatedly shamed in early life become shame-based. Shame becomes part of the individual's identity. Shame is the belief that, "I am a flawed human being."

In Dr. Bradshaw's book, Healing the Shame that Binds You, he
is quoted as saying:

"If our primary caregivers are shame-based, they will act
shameless and pass their toxic shame onto us. There is no way to
teach self-value if one does not value oneself. Toxic shame is
multigenerational. It is passed from one generation to the next.
Shame-based people find other shame-based people and get
married. As each member of a couple carries the shame from his
or her own family system, their marriage will be grounded in
their shame-core. The major outcome of this will be a lack of
intimacy. It's difficult to let someone get close to you if you feel
defective and flawed as a human being. Shame-based couples
maintain non-intimacy through poor communication,
nonproductive circular fighting, games, manipulation, vying for
control, withdrawal, blaming and confluence. Confluence is the
agreement never to disagree. Confluence creates pseudo-
intimacy."

How do we know when the shame we are feeling is toxic and
when it is not? The litmus test for shame is to ask yourself, is the
shame I feel helping deal well in life or is it running every aspect
of who I am.

Incidences of Non-Toxic and Toxic Shame

For instance, you are in a friend relationship with another and
you get annoyed when they are late. You put up with their poor
behavior for weeks, but one day you lash out at them without
warning. Afterwards, you feel ashamed of how you treated your
friend, and call them to humbly apologize for your actions and
ask them to forgive you.

This is an example of non-toxic shame that is helping you to
deal with another in a relationship.

Now let's look at two incidences of toxic shame in action.

Incidence One: You have good friend who you know has just
received a much-deserved promotion and pay raise from the
company where you both are employed. Instead of feeling happy
and congratulating her for her accomplishment, you feel angry

and insolent. So, when you hear two co-workers discussing their amazement at her promotion, you join in the conversation telling them private things about your friend's life that you should not expose. Soon the office is buzzing with the information you shared. Your friend hears the rumors and learns you are the source and confronts you for what you did. Instead of reacting with humility and apologizing, you lash out and angrily deny the accusations. You part ways with your friend and find a new job because you cannot allow yourself to admit to yourself or others that you made a mistake.

Clearly, the toxic shame from your past fogged your ability to deal with current shame appropriately and toxic shame is running your life.

Incidence Two: You have been invited to the birthday of a close friend and she informs you that at the also invited to the party is a very nice person she things would make a great partner for you. The morning of the party you get up and go into the bathroom to take a shower and see yourself in the mirror. You stand there for several minutes feeling deeply ashamed at your appearance and decide to call your friend and take a rain check on her invitation.

The self-loathing you felt while looking in the mirror was an echo of the way your parents and friends from childhood made you feel. They said you were fat, ugly and those messages became cemented in your mind and now you believe them to be true.

Toxic shame can also underlie a constant need to impress other people and never, ever be wrong.

Also, toxic shame also leads to self-loathing, depression, suicidal ideation and actions.

Toxic shame can run our lives by coloring our thinking and behaviors.

The Four Requirements to Overcome Toxic Shame

In former pieces, we have examined neuroplasticity and how we can change our brains by changing our actions. Basically, fake it until you make it activity.

Thankfully our brains are pliable, and we can teach it new ways of functioning and train our minds to think more positively and change our lives.

Healing from toxic shame is no different.

To heal our brains and thus our minds from toxic shame, there are four different tasks we must cultivate.

The first is to develop self-love. Developing self-compassion sounds easier than it is in practice as we have grown up believing such negative messages. However, it is vital if we are to conquer toxic shame.

Next, we need to listen to what we are saying, both verbally and non-verbally the words we use in our dialogue to ourselves.

Third, we need to mourn the wounds from our past. This includes the ability to identify what happened and how those past hurts are affecting how we feel about ourselves.

Last, we need to learn self-forgiveness. No, we did not harm ourselves nor did we give ourselves toxic shame. However, we have done many things since we became adults that have further harmed us such as drug or alcohol use or allowing ourselves to remain in toxic relationships. It's time to forgive ourselves and to move on.

Doing these fake-it-until-we-make-it fundamentals can start us on our way to conquering toxic shame.

Therapeutic Aspects of Conquering Toxic Shame

Toxic shame is caused by so many different types of harm by others that one might think there is not a single option that can help. While it is for sure that people are different in the length of time it will take to overcome toxic shame, the basics are the same for each of us.

First, let me say here and now that if you are dealing with toxic shame you will most likely need a mental health professional to successfully heal. Find a counselor that is a good fit and it would help greatly if they are trauma-informed. However, I understand very well that trauma-informed therapists are hard to come by in rural America, but at least find someone who you feel cares for you as a person.

After finding your mental health professional, here are the three very helpful aspects to conquering toxic shame once and for all. While reading these suggestions, examine how they fit into the four requirements listed above.

Rewrite History. I'm not suggesting here that you can literally go back in time and change history. However, what I am saying is you can rewrite what happened to you in childhood on paper and in your mind.

With your therapist, choose one of the experiences from your childhood where you were made to feel ashamed of your body (or other memory). Think of how you would rewrite that scene.

For me, I went back in time and, as my adult self, rescued me from that situation. I told my childhood self that I was taking her home with me and that she would never feel ashamed like that again. I removed her from the care of the parents who shamed me and took her home and continued to tell her how pretty she was and how much I loved her.

I didn't do this extremely powerful exercise just once, but over and again until my inner child felt happy because she knew she was safe, loved and most of all, unashamed.

Allow others to compliment you. To begin this exercise, pretend someone is complimenting you on how pretty you are and any other attribute you can think of about yourself. Allow yourself to hear the words and notice how good they make you feel.

Then the next time someone gives you a compliment, do not allow it to just roll off your back or make an excuse to them why it is not true. Instead, allow their words to enter your consciousness and relish in them. Thank them warmly for their kindness and enjoy the moment.

Do mirror work. Stand before a mirror and take a real good look at yourself. I mean all of you! Take a hand mirror and lay on your bed naked and look at yourself.

Pay attention to the fact that you are a woman/man, not a monster or ugly like you thought. No matter how big or small you are or any scars you see, you are a human being, no more, no less.

It is NOT a sin to love yourself, all of you, flaws and all.

I won't lie to you, this is extremely hard at first. When my therapist encouraged me to do this, I couldn't for several weeks. However, once I did I made an amazing discovery.

I'm not an ogre nor am I someone who needs to be locked up. I am a flawed human being just like everybody else.

In Conclusion

I realize that toxic shame is telling you that you don't deserve to heal. It is a liar. You are worthy of self-love, respect and dignity just as every human being on planet earth.

The messages you were told in childhood need not control who you are today. Like any words in any message, the negative ones should be and can be changed into positive messages of love and self-acceptance.

It may take some time, but the release and joy that follows conquering toxic shame is amazing.

In our next piece, we will bring all we have discovered and discussed about toxic shame together. In the meantime, say something lovely to yourself because you deserve it.

Dissociation: In Laymen's Terms

There are many terms in psychology which, if you are not in the know, may seem obscure or strange. In my experience in speaking with in public, dissociation is one that many folks have never heard of or are confused by. That's why I decided to attempt to write an explanation of this term in my own words. I can only speak from a non-professional stance as one who has lived experience with Dissociative Identity Disorder, the most extreme expression of what is a normal human behavior when confronted with overwhelming experiences.

Dissociation isn't an unusual or unhealthy mental mechanism. It is something all humans experience. A common incidence people may have of dissociation is what I have termed the movie theater experience.

A Common Form of Dissociation Verses Clinical Dissociation

You go to the theater to see a movie you have been anticipating seeing for months. You sit down in an empty row with your popcorn and soda and the movie starts. Soon you get involved with the film, so much so that you lose all concept of time. After the movie, you become aware that there are people sitting beside you and that you have eaten your popcorn and drank your soda. You have no recollection of the other people seating themselves beside you or of your eating and drinking your treats.

This is a common form of dissociation.

Dissociation is just a fancy word for "checking out". When I dissociate I become disconnected from my thoughts, feelings, memories and who I am. In this condition, one of my ego states comes forward and lives my life for me to protect me from what I have determined to be overwhelming circumstances.

These ego states are found in every human, however in most people they can communicate with one another forming a running narrative of the events in one's life. In my case, my ego states have been separated by amnesiac walls which I began to form in early childhood, which prevent communication.

So, when faced with something I feel overcome by, one of my separated ego states becomes energized and takes over. When I am "checked out", I am dissociated.

Dissociation as a Coping Mechanism

Dissociation can be a wonderful coping mechanism when one is in danger, however it can be destructive. In my life living with Dissociative Identity Disorder, it has destroyed friendships, romantic relationships, jobs, and many other aspects of life that most people take for granted.

Because I lose my sense of right and wrong with some of my alter ego states, I have been in trouble with the police and had to declare bankruptcy due to credit cards that I normally would never have gotten, let alone used. I got married in a dissociated state, literally waking up next to a man on our wedding night. As one can see, it is not a disorder to be desired.

One aspect of dissociation I should like to speak about is who and what these alter ego states are and are not. They are parts of me, fragmented parts of my personality. They ARE NOT different personalities. They ARE NOT, or could they ever become monsters such as was portrayed in a recent popular movie.

They do not possess supernatural strength, (such as the ability to climb walls), nor are they violent.

Being dissociated does not make me dangerous or more likely to commit a heinous crime. It is a coping and defense mechanism, nothing more, nothing less.

What Does Clinical Dissociation Feel Like

I will give one more explanation to what dissociation feels like. It is one that most Americans have experienced at least once, especially in our adolescent or early adulthood years.

You go out drinking with your friends and get wasted. After a while you black out. You wake up the next day and your friends begin telling you about all the things you said and did the night before but which you have absolutely no memory of saying or doing.

This is what it feels like to dissociate, only it happens to me every day. It is not fun, it is not something to be desired, and more understanding of what dissociation is needs to be spread among the public so that movies and television programs that attempt to use dissociation to sell movie tickets and advertising spots lose their flavor.

People with dissociative disorders are not weird or strange, we are ordinary people who have taken our human ability to escape overwhelming trauma to the next level.

Perhaps this last statement is the most important point I wish to get across to all who read anything I read.

"Beneath the surface of the protective parts of trauma survivors there exists an undamaged essence, a Self that is confident, curious, and calm, a Self that has been sheltered from destruction by the various protectors that have emerged in their efforts to ensure survival. Once those protectors trust that it is safe to separate, the Self-will spontaneously emerge, and the parts can be enlisted in the healing process" ~ Bessel A. van der Kolk, The Body Keeps the Score: Brain, Mind, and Body in the Healing of Trauma

Escaping from the Cage of Childhood Trauma

I've spent a lot of time trapped in my own morass of emotions. True, the traumatic things that happened in my childhood first put me in the quagmire of self-pity and fear I have lived in, but later in life I chose of my own volition to remain there. As an adult, I found myself trapped in a prison of my own making, unable to escape and indeed lacking the desire to do so.

I understand that saying that living as a person with the persona of victim isn't good, may wrinkle a few eyebrows. I remember the since of entitlement I felt when I began to work on these issues, and how I felt the world "owed me". I'm here now to say that those emotions are bogus and will only serve to trap a person further in the hell the trauma forced them into.

Living in a Cage

There is a quality to living in a cage that many do not comprehend. One can become so comfortable living in it, that we lose the desire to flee. There is an identity to being someone in captivity, and letting go of that identity, no matter how painful it is, takes courage. One may wonder how such misery as self-doubt, isolation and loneliness can become someone's identity and their comfort zone. Like living in a cage, one can lose sight that there is anything else.

We get used to the limitations we ourselves have set up, and fear going beyond the boundaries of our misery. Who are we without our anger and bitterness? Don't we deserve to feel depressed and anxious?

I remember well my first years in psychotherapy. I wore the identity of a victim of childhood trauma like a crown. This self-imposed label set me apart in my mind, making me special and different from those who had not experienced the things I had when young. It made me haughty in a sort of strange way, as though I was somehow superior to others due to my traumatic past.

I placed myself upon a pedestal, like a queen expecting others to kowtow to my eccentricities and bad behavior. It took a wonderful therapist and some hard introspection to find out that not only was I in this cage, but that it counterproductive to be living there. No matter how comfortable I was in my gloom, it wasn't better than living life with purpose and acceptance.

The first step in leaving the cage of childhood trauma is to acknowledge that you are indeed enclosed in one. This takes some honest introspection. I did my self-searching with a therapist who refused to allow me to behave like a spoiled brat in her presence.

More than once she pointed out to me how I was responsible for my behavior, no matter what had happened to make me upset. It was during this stage that I began to acknowledge that not all my childhood experiences were horrendous, not even with those who harmed me. There had been fun times too.

This was a new thought, and it gave me strength to go forward knowing that I wasn't some total freak who had been raised by outlandishly crazy people. In fact, I had to acknowledge that those beliefs were totally false.

The next step is to consider leaving. This step may seem obvious, but it is perhaps the hardest. One must be able to visualize what it would be like not to be closed-up in one's own misery and what how life would be different.

To progress, I had to consider looking outside my circle of injured acquaintances, to people who had not been traumatized as children. I was then able to pay attention to how they conducted their lives, and to see what they experienced that I might desire to take on as my own. I found that these folks smiled a lot and talked with energy about the small things in their lives that made them happy.

They didn't spend large amounts of time talking about the past, but rather enjoyed conversing about their children, their pets and their social lives. It wasn't long before I too desired to enjoy peace, laughter and companionship, things located outside my cage.

The last step was to step outside my cage and experience freedom. The fear that leaving the confines of my cage of discouragement and isolation is hard to describe.

At first, I thought the anxiety would destroy me, however after I had taken my first tentative steps, I knew I would never go back. The air outside the cage, full of heartache and tears, is sweet beyond compare.

The colors are brighter, the sounds are clearer, and I have been enjoying living so much more. Beyond the confines of my cage, there were relationships and plans to be made for my future. I was afraid at first of those two things, but slowly I began to relish in being able to make both.

I know I've been speaking in symbolic language, and it may sound like I have managed to escape my cage successfully without too many hitches. Nothing could be farther from the truth.

It took me almost three decades of hard work to get where I am today, and I still run into my cage and hide sometimes. I'm still learning how to cope with life on life's terms, but by God I'm here and I'm not going to ever allow myself to live in a prison again.

I invite all who have lived in their own cages of self-pity, self-doubt, and entitlement to come out here where the air is fresh and clean. Yes, there are traumatic events out here too. It is impossible to live life without difficulties or running into people who are disagreeable.

However, I would much rather live out here in the world than to
be trapped in my own misery.

"There is freedom waiting for you, on the breezes of the sky.
You may ask, "What if I fall?"
I can only answer,
"Oh, my darling, what if you fly?"
~Erin Hanson

Four Reasons Dissociative Identity Disorder is Controversial Among Mental Health Professionals

As any of you who have read this blog know, I live with a condition known as Dissociative Identity Disorder, what was once known as Multiple Personality Disorder. DID is a very controversial diagnosis among the professionals of the mental health field and I believe I have identified some of the reasons for this. Four of the primary causes of this inability of some mental health professionals to accept the diagnosis of Dissociative Identity Disorder fall into four categories: The DSM criteria, disbelief, misinformation and fear.

Dissociative Identity Disorder in the DSM-5

The first reason I shall speak about is the DSM criteria.

"The existence of two or more distinct identities (or "personality states"). The distinct identities are accompanied by changes in behavior, memory and thinking. The signs and symptoms may be observed by others or reported by the individual.

Ongoing gaps in memory about everyday events, personal information and/or past traumatic events.
The symptoms cause significant distress or problems in social, occupational or other areas of functioning."

While this does explain very well the majority of the symptoms involved with DID, it causes many problems for clinicians too. How do you determine the existence of two or more distinct

identities with changes in behavior etc. when your client doesn't
present them? Presenting my alters to a therapist or a
Psychiatrist, or anyone for that matter, isn't as simple as it may
seem on the surface. I must truly trust someone before they will
be aware that I have switched.

I saw the same therapist for many, many years and trusted her
more than anyone in the entire world, yet she only met four of
my ego states in all that time. The likelihood of a relative
stranger meeting them is slim to none. The trap that many
clinicians fall into is that they believe they must see the alter
states for themselves before they can diagnose someone with
this disorder.

All of Psychiatry is Self-Reported.

I have been told by several well-meaning Psychiatrists that they
could not in all good conscious give me the diagnosis of
Dissociative Identity Disorder (although I had been diagnosed
by other professionals) without meeting the others. When
confronted by a professional with their inability to diagnose
without seeing, I simply remind them that all mental health
disorders are self-reported. There is no empirical proof, in fact,
that mental disorders even exist.

All of psychiatry is self-reported.

The disbelief I am speaking about in my opening paragraph is
the disbelief that such horrendous things, such as are reported by
people like myself living with DID, happen to children. No
human, unless they are completely heartless, wants to believe
that the atrocities reported to have been committed against
survivors could have happened. Denial of these truths is one of
the primary causes of the painful denial among survivors. Who
on earth would want to admit to themselves that caregivers could
do such horrendous things to innocents. Unfortunately, it does
and will continue to happen until we get child abuse out in the
open and have a dialogue about it as a society.

The third cause, I have determined to be the continual mill of
disinformation pouring out of the media about DID. There are
movies and television shows that sensationalize and demonize

people like myself. If you have seen any of these films and programs, you will know what I mean. I have been asked if I have supernatural abilities like the ability to climb walls, and if any of my alters are dangerous. Public opinion is shaped by the media, and clinicians are no different.

This continual assault on the realities of living with DID is more than unfortunate. It makes the diagnosis seem unreal and many clinicians are swayed while the media continues to use Dissociative Identity Disorder to make money hand over fist.

Therapists Risk Their Professional Reputation

The last of my thoughts on why professionals have such a hard time believing in DID is that they are afraid. The stigma involved with Dissociative Identity Disorder doesn't just involve the people who must live with it, it spills over into the professional world as well.

To believe in and treat DID is to risk your reputation among other clinicians. This is so unfortunate. We need open minds to honestly and openly work on this problem without fear of reprisal in any way. Only then can the victims of severe trauma who have developed the capacity to dissociate receive fair and lasting treatment.

The main reason I write this blog and my books is to help change the public and professional opinion about what Dissociative Identity Disorder is like and how to treat it. I am not a superhuman nor am I a monster. I am an ordinary person who was exposed to extremely harmful abuse as a child and learned to use my natural human ability to dissociate to survive.

"Life is inherently risky. There is only one big risk you should avoid at all costs, and that is the risk of doing nothing." ~ Denis Waitley

Learning to Live with Dissociative Identity Disorder

People living with DID, like myself, often know all our lives that something isn't quite right about how we experience the world. We have experienced the effects of amnesia in relationships with friends and family.

In this article, we will discover together how to learn to live with dissociative identity disorder.

Buried Memories and Seeking Help

We who live with the diagnosis of DID have faced severe episodes of depression and anxiety without understanding why. These things often come to a head when our brains reach maturity and the memories so carefully stored away burst into our consciousness.

These buried memories and the knowledge of the existence of alternate ego states are, at first, overwhelming to us as memories of the trauma from the past come up voluntarily and uncontrollably.

The chaos of living with the flashbacks and all the other chaos has often become difficult, exasperating, and sometimes dangerous.

I say dangerous because the emotions, flashbacks, and the feelings of worthlessness and helpless can drive us to feel suicidal and many of attempt to end our lives.

Unfortunately, many succeed.

It is at this point that many of us seek professional help.

The Grieving Process

Thus, a grieving process begins.

We grieve for the loss of what we had always thought was a
normal childhood. We are forced to face the reality that we had
suppressed, that our early lives were marked by unspeakable acts
perpetrated against us by people we knew and loved.

During this upheaval, we begin because we must learn coping
and grounding skills to deal with the memories and flashbacks.
As we work, and each memory is worked through, it slowly
loses its power and fades into the past where it belongs.

Reaching out to others who have also experienced childhood
trauma is central at this stage of change do to the loneliness and
isolation we experience.

Sharing with others who understand our pain helps us in
accepting that dissociative identity disorder is not a "weird"
diagnosis, but rather the logical outcome of early childhood
trauma.

Dependence on Our Therapists

Inevitably, as we struggle with the severe issues that accompany
dissociative identity disorder, we will grow in dependence on
our therapists. This is not harmful if the professional that is
helping us is well-seasoned and aware of this propensity by
adults who faced horrendous abuse in childhood.

After facing what happened to us and experiencing the emotions
that accompany them, we can begin the process of accepting
who we are today. However, we face a struggle, as we will want
to go back into the denial from which we have emerged because
of the pain of facing the truth.

However, once we accept that our past experiences are not the ruin of us, but what has made us the resilient human beings we have become, we grow in our self-image and self-esteem.

There comes a day when we decide we have relived all we need to understand well what happened in our childhoods, and how the event have shaped us today. It is during this time that we make the choice to allow the past to fade into the background and become part of who are and not our entire identity.

The Two Biggest Misunderstandings About DID

There are two beliefs among those who do not fully understand dissociative identity disorder that seem to permeate both professional and popular literature.

One is that a person living with dissociative identity disorder, like myself, are totally unaware until entering therapy that there are alters. While this may be the so in a small number of cases, it is not true for most of us. While we who are diagnosed in therapy with dissociative identity disorder may not understand what has been happening to us, we know that there have been many incidences in our lives where unexplainable events have occurred.

For instance, someone states with fury that we have done something we do not remember having done.

The second misunderstanding it is only after treatment begins that the memories of childhood trauma surface.

Again, this may be so for some cases but the reason we begin seeking help is because we are having flashbacks and emotional outbursts. We ask seek help because we feel severely depressed and anxious without apparent cause.

I began to suspect that the way I saw things and lived wasn't "normal" and that something in my past had caused the lack of peace I felt.

Reaching A Milestone

Finally, after many years of hard work, trauma, and drama we
will begin to seek a future free of their past. This is a significant
milestone in our healing.

We have reached a compromise within their selves where one
alter is the leader and cooperation begins in earnest. All our
personality, while not consolidated, work together for the
common cause of a happy and fulfilling life.

**My Experience with Entering Therapy and Learning to Live
with DID**

My suspicion began young.

I had many things happen to me that didn't compute. My little
friends would complain that I had done things or said things I
just didn't remember, and I felt lost and alone. I would sit for
hours and contemplate my behavior feeling puzzled.

My friends were so adamant that I had done those things, but the
actions didn't fit my usual self, and I just couldn't understand. I
spent hours at a time lost in my little world, spaced out so far
that I was unaware of my surroundings.

My teachers complained that I daydreamed a lot, but I knew I
wasn't thinking or fantasizing about anything during those
times. I was just simply not there.

When I began having horrendous flashbacks at age twenty-nine
and felt overwhelmingly depressed and anxious, I sought
professional help. I began seeing a highly trained therapist who
did some careful observations of me during our sessions.

I had a hard time staying in the room with her and didn't
remember even going to our sessions for the first several months
we met. It was frustrating and frightening to me that I had no
memory of driving to and from her office, or that I had even
attending those office visits.

After a period of several months I point-blank asked her what was wrong with me and she carefully and quietly told me she believed I may be living with a problem called (at that time) multiple personality disorder.

While I was floored by this diagnosis, I was also relieved. As we discussed what DID was, I felt relieved at finally understanding the strange occurrences that had plagued me all my life.

It was after I began to understand myself, that I wasn't crazy but experiencing the effects of childhood trauma, that the healing could begin.

After many years of arduous work with my therapist, I have now reached a point in my healing where I experience more peace than ever in my life. Yes, I still experience flashbacks, but now I understand that they cannot harm me. The memories the flashbacks represent are not in the present but in the past.

I have fully accepted my diagnosis and myself and can now move forward.

My internal system has become self-aware and we are moving quickly towards fusion. Life is good, but it took time and patience with myself to get here.

Like my therapist Paula did for me, I believe in you for you because I know you too can find the peace I have found by learning to accept my diagnosis and who I am.

I wish you good luck on your healing journey.

"You can't go back and change the beginning, but you can start where you are and change the ending." ~ C.S. Lewis

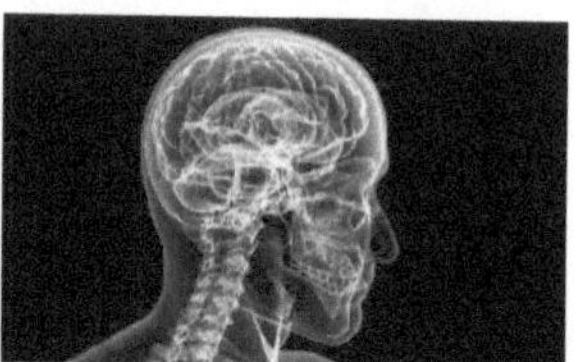

Living with Dissociative Amnesia

Remembering yesterday comes easily for most adults. They can recall events and details about where they were and whom they met with relative ease, even after several days have passed. It is not so with people like me, who live with the amnesia that accompanies dissociative identity disorder.

Amnesia in My Life

All my life I've been painfully aware that I do not remember things like everyone else. There have always been huge gaps in my mind of not just learned knowledge from school, but also personal events, places, and people. At one time, I put these anomalies off to a bad memory, but now I know it is a functional form of amnesia.

I seem to be adept at selecting which things I wish to remember and which I don't. I do not remember names, but I do remember faces and voices. I do remember odd trivia facts but bless me if I can remember events from yesterday experiences good or bad.

People Aren't Aware

People around me are unaware of this problem. I have become very good at playing along so that they do not catch on. When I meet someone in a store that obviously knows me, I can carry on a nonsense conversation, and they be totally unaware that I just faked my way through.

As time goes on, I have become increasingly aware to just how this quirk in my cognitive ability plays out. I seem to experience life as a bunch of new beginnings. I tend to push away experiences, good or bad, into a corner of my mind and move forward without giving what just occurred anymore thought.

I Cannot Retrieve My Memories

While this was adaptive as a child experiencing severe and repeated childhood trauma, it has become a severe handicap in adult life.

I long to remember from one day to the next the important things done the day before. I do have an overarching memory of the basic facts, such as I went to school, and I took an exam, but the details of who was there and sometimes what day it was on are lost. More to the point, I am unable to retrieve them.
I could go into the neuroscience behind this phenomenon, but I'll spare you that this time around.

What is important is that I am aware that I don't hold onto information and that I do it on purpose.

I Would Love to Remember

I hear people online talking about how fearful they are because they suffer from amnesia, but why be afraid? It is a tool that has served us well for many years and is the reason we are not insane from the tragedies of our childhoods.

Would I like to be aware of my movements and actions from day to day? Sure. However, I must be patient and understanding with myself. Amnesia served was a way to remain alive and hopeful in a horrifically demanding and ego destroying environment when I was young.

Had I not been given the ability to "forget" the hopelessness and helplessness would have destroyed me. As it was, I did try to kill myself at age six, and being able to push the despair I must have felt to the back burner of my mind helped me to survive.

For now, I am at a loss as to how to change this ingrained and subconscious behavior. So, I have decided to accept amnesia as an annoying yet understandable part of my life's experience. It is part of who I am, not my identity, and I do find in getting along in life, and that is what matters.

Words of Wisdom

My words of wisdom for anyone who understands what I am
speaking of are these:
Don't be afraid of something that has helped you for so long.
Yes, it is exacerbating, but it is not harmful. It's okay. Really.
Fighting against this adaptation is fighting against all the things
that have helped you survive. Instead, learn to use this ability
and relax.

Nothing serious ever got better by worrying or complaining
about it. In fact, stewing on forgetting can and often does make
things worse.

Accept who you are flaws and all. You'll find that life gets a lot
easier and the world will seem a safer place to remember.

"Fear keeps us focused on the past or worried about the future. If
we can acknowledge our fear, we can realize that right now we
are okay.

Right now, today, we are still alive, and our bodies are working
marvelously. Our eyes can still see the beautiful sky. Our ears
can still hear the voices of our loved ones." Thich Nhat Hanh

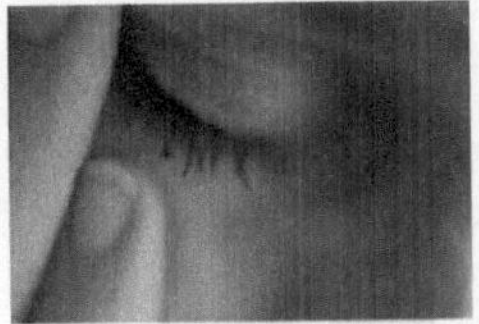

The Painful Phenomenon of Switching Headaches

A somewhat common problem for people living with dissociative identity disorder is switching headaches. While they do not occur in everyone who lives with DID, they are a painful reminder to many that they are burdened with the disorder.

Even though I have been in therapy for thirty years now, if I come under enough stress I will switch alters. I am co-conscious with my others, so I am aware of what is being said and done, but just barely. To be clear, it takes an enormous amount of internal or external stress to cause me fall back on the default behavior of switching.

I am going to write this piece about my own experiences with these often-debilitating apparitions.

Real Headaches Vs. Fake Ones

Believe it or not, these switching headaches have an official name. Transitional Interpersonality Thunderclap Headaches (TITH). There is no known understanding of how or why these painful migraines occur. The research I read stated that after a thorough neurological examination during the time a TITH was happening showed no irregularities whatsoever leaving the researchers scratching their heads.

When I was growing up, I was sent to several neurologists because of the blinding headaches I experienced every day, often several times a day. I would be fine one moment, then have the sudden onset of a terrible migraine that could last anywhere from a few minutes to several hours. They did several batteries of tests, including a particularly nasty one called a pneumoencephalogram, sure they would find a lesion or tumor, but they found nothing.

At one point they even decided I was faking the headaches to gain attention, but that was soon laid to rest. They placed me in the hospital and observed me closely, careful not to let me know they were doing so. When one of these horrifically painful events occurred, I was alone and did not look for someone to help me. They saw me change moods suddenly, then grab my head and rock, apparently in agony.

Looking back, I know what was happening. I was switching a lot back then. The trauma was ongoing that caused DID to develop in my mind, and the switching was very intense. The doctors in the 1960s were unaware of the trauma I was living in and had little to no knowledge of dissociative identity disorder. Even less than many doctors know today.

My Recent History with Switching Headaches

Recently, I was having a crisis of significant proportions. I immediately began to experience severe headaches that nothing would help. They were worse than migraines, (if that is possible), and I was more miserable than I had been with just the crisis.

The only way I could resolve both problems was by seeing my therapist and pouring out to her all I was feeling. While speaking to her my head was throbbing, and I felt myself switching moods rapidly, but I kept on talking and cursing.

After raving for forty-five minutes, I felt much, much better.

I took a deep breath and looked at my therapist who was sitting quietly nearby clearly stunned by what she had just witnessed. I smiled sheepishly and said,

"Well, now I think you've met just about the whole gang."

Her response was priceless. She sat back, smiled and said, "So I have."

Now, I realize that pouring out one's guts to a therapist may not be the answer for every circumstance nor is it for everyone. I only know that venting that day released an enormous amount of pressure off my mind, and I am again able to function.

The main point of this post is to say that migraines caused by switching, especially rapid switching, is not abnormal and should not cause you to fear. Yes, please, have yourself thoroughly examined by your doctor, but don't be surprised if they find nothing physically wrong.

Switching headaches, I could sure live without them.

"I wear my personality on my sleeve, for sure, and my look is constantly changing because so am I." Halsey

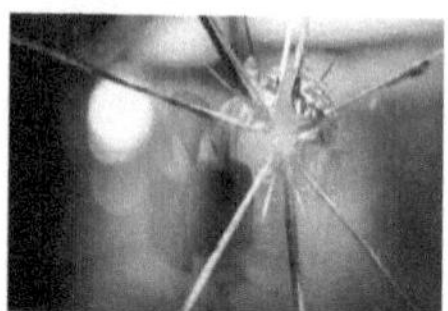

Choosing to Remain a Victim

I know from experience and from my observations of others
living with the after-effects of childhood trauma, that at first, we
identify as victims. We spend an inordinate amount of time
feeling sorry for ourselves and believe in our hearts that we will
forever be relegated to the corridors of victimhood.

I have experienced and firmly believe there is something beyond
being a victim and that's what I'm discussing here today.

What Do We Gain from Remaining a Victim

By maintaining the identity of victim, people who maintain this
identity are protected from ever having to engage life and its
hurdles.

They do this by avoiding taking responsibility for their lives,
choosing to remain a perpetual victim.

The belief systems of the person with a victim identity fall along
these lines:

- I am broken
- I am damaged goods
- My life is too difficult
- My life is harder anyone else's
- I shouldn't try because I'll fail
- I must remain on alert because others only want to hurt
  me

- I cannot and must not trust anyone
- I know that everyone else has it better and they don't want to help me
- I'm a victim, I deserve for others to take care of me
- The rules don't pertain to me, I'm a victim
- No one else understands just how hard it is to be a victim like me
- I deserve your help, but you better not try because you'll fail
- The best thing for me to do is never believe I'll get better because then people will feel sorry for me

People with a victim identity will complain to others about how hard their life has become, but if anyone offers them options on how to change they are met with negative responses.

They ask for help, but when you offer it they find a way to sabotage the help you give and then complain their failure was your fault.

God forbid you should tell them the truth about what you see, that they deliberately failed, because they will become hostile and decide you are not a friend and ignore you.

However, maybe weeks or months later, when they want something from you, they return acting like nothing happened.

Victims will hold onto anger and seek pity from others. They get angry because others "don't understand me" or they hurl insults saying you are being, "condescending and invalidating" their emotions and what they went through.

Victims see no need to be grateful for what they have, and scoff when someone gives them a compliment because they cannot allow someone to believe in them.

That would be way too risky.

A Secondary Gain for Remaining a Victim

Because they identify as victims, these folks feel entitled and will use others to get their way and meet their needs.

Victims bully others using guilt and tears to get others to provide financial support and make the hard choices for them. However, they resent the help they receive, and the decisions made by others for them.

The Victim typically knows exactly what buttons to push in others to get them to begin or continue to take care of them.

Often the person identifying as a victim will retreat into his victim mentality to justify his abuse of others. Victims wholeheartedly believe that life is harder for them than for anyone else, and they either do not recognize or wish to support you when you are having difficulties yourself.

The victim believes uses the rationale they cannot and do not deserve a better life than they have now to not take responsibility for their own lives or their actions.

It is difficult for the victim to see that they are living as a victim instead of living the life they could. This is because they are full of shame and attempt to manipulate their history falsely building up their accomplishment while avoiding speaking of their failures.

Changing Directions

It takes a huge leap for someone with this mentality to recognize that being a victim isn't desirable and they should choose a different path. Changing the direction of one's life takes an understanding that they can change their behavior patterns and take control of their lives because they are strong and capable human beings.

In short, they do not need to remain victims any longer, but can become survivors.

However, the truth is that he must keep believing that or they firmly believe that their lives will get harder.

"Being a survivor doesn't mean being strong - it's telling people when you need a meal or a ride, company, whatever. It's paying attention to heart wisdom, feelings, not living a role, but having a unique, authentic life, having something to contribute, finding time to love and laugh. All these things are qualities of survivors." ~ Bernie Siegel

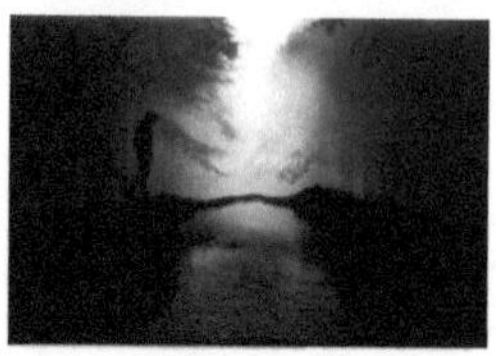

Making the Choice to Get Well

Making the decision to get well may sound like an easy task but making the decision to get well is something that unfortunately many people never do. I'm not sure what helps one person to see they have a problem and become determined to work on it and another to choose to live a chaotic and unfulfilled life.

In fact, according to my therapist, specialists have been debating that subject for decades.

All I know is that somewhere down inside myself there was a deep curiosity as to what living a life relatively free of excessive trauma and drama was like.

The day I entered my Therapist's office for the first time I really had no concept of how sick I truly had become. I was losing time, had huge memory losses and other aberrations but I honestly thought that everyone did.

I was like a woman who had been blind from birth suddenly realizing the darkness I had always experienced was not what everyone else saw.

Those first years of therapy were pure hell as the memories of what had happened to me as a child accompanied by the inevitable denial that those things could never happen to anyone kept me in a constant state of turmoil.
So many times, I wanted to give up but Paula, that's my therapist's name, urged me on and at one point she asked me, "Do you want the bastards to win?"

Those became fighting words that spurred me on. What kept me choosing to go on instead of self-destructing as I had been programmed to do, because I had told the horrible family secrets?

Perhaps my tenacity or just plain down right stubbornness I don't know.

In my entries to this blog I am going to share the different methods I have employed to get and stay sane and in control of my life.

Some of it will be hard to read because I will be real about the obstacles I have faced. I tell you this though, against seemingly insurmountable odds I have survived the evil actions of my abusers in my past and the trauma/drama of recovery.

I am now thriving and loving every minutes of every day. Even the bad things that come into my life such as sickness and disappointment are beautiful in contrast to the living death I was existing in before I got into therapy.

I wish to thank Dave for this opportunity to speak out on issues that are dear to my heart, the main one being that I wish to pull as many people along with me who will come down the road to recovery.

In future entries I will tell you about those early days of chaos, what it is like to live in and leave an Inpatient Psychiatric Facility, returning to school at age 54 and many, many other topics.

I will make you this promise, there is an end to it.

The crying will stop, the flashbacks will get better and you will emerge from the other side of the turmoil of recovery stronger and more persistent than ever.

The pain will not go on forever and one day you will awaken and realize you have had more good days than bad that week.

"When something bad happens you have three choices, you can let it define you, you can let it destroy you, or you can let it strengthen you." ~ Author Unknown

The Huge Treatment Problems When Treating People with the Diagnosis of Dissociative Identity Disorder

Having received treatment in therapy for DID for over 29 years, I am in a unique position to write about some of the tough issues we who live with the disorder face. These problems and the traps one can fall into during healing is the main reason I write In a Nutshell.

In this article, I'm not going to explain each issue, I'm going to give you a list. My purpose isn't to discourage anyone, but to shed light on why healing from DID takes so long and why it can be a dangerous path.

What I have discovered is that, although the travels I have made on the road to healing, all the pain and hard work has been well worth it.

The Treatment Issues of Healing from Dissociative Identity Disorder

- Stabilization of the person – both internally and externally
- Managing and eliminating self-injury and self-harm issues
- Examining and obtaining current-day external safety from abuse
- Internal system safety
- Developing effective internal communication

- Calming internal noise and chaos
- Working specifically with child parts
- Working specifically with adult parts
- Working specifically with teenage parts
- Learning about the other system parts
- Working with internal perpetrator introjects
- Creating emotional separation from external perpetrators
- Working with triggers
- Correcting cognitive distortions
- Addressing gender confusion, male vs. female issues
- Processing emotions
- Body image issues
- Reducing time loss, memory loss, amnesia
- Time confusion, time distortion
- Trauma processing – memory work
- Body memories and kinesthetic issues
- Understanding re-enactments and trauma bonds
- Healing sexual abuse issues
- Healing physical abuse issues
- Healing emotional abuse issues
- Healing ritualized abuse issues
- Healing exploitation, pornography, prostitution, sex slavery issues
- Managing family, marital, parenting issues
- Addressing addictions
- Managing eating disorders
- Household management issues – improving daily functioning
- Relationship issues and teaching social skills
- Understanding the effects of trauma on the brain
- Improving self-independence and self-reliance
- Improving self-esteem issues
- Leaving disability and regaining employment
- Depression and medication management
- Bipolar disorder and medication management
- Anxiety / Panic and medication management
- Complex Post-traumatic stress issues (CPTSD)

- Reducing phobias
- Social anxiety and social isolation
- Safely eliminating suicidal ideation and suicidal behaviors
- Homicidal ideation and anger management
- Exploring spiritual confusion
- Philosophical issues
- Detachment and separation issues
- Treating sleep disorders
- Treating medical complications and physical harm resulting from the abuse
- Reaching integration, blended states, or effective system team work
- Getting past denial

Whew!

A dream doesn't become reality through magic; it takes sweat, determination and hard work.
~ Colin Powell

A Glossary of Terms to Help You Understand Dissociative Identity Disorder Better

Alter- an ego state that has been separated from other ego states by amnesiac barriers which began to be formed in very early childhood.

Anxiety Disorder – an anxiety disorder is described as having problems having intense, excessive and persistent worry and fear about everyday situations. Often, anxiety disorders involve repeated episodes of sudden feelings of intense anxiety and fear or terror that reach a peak within minutes (panic attacks). These feelings of anxiety and panic interfere with daily activities, are difficult to control, are out of proportion to the actual danger and can last a long time. You may avoid places or situations to prevent these feelings. Symptoms may start during childhood or the teen years and continue into adulthood.

Attachment Disorder-defined as the condition in which individuals have difficulty forming lasting relationships. They often show nearly a complete lack of ability to be genuinely affectionate with others. They typically fail to develop a conscience and do not learn to trust.

Big- This a term people who live with dissociative identity disorder use to describe the adult members of their multiple system.

Body Memory- Memories aren't only stored in the thinking part of the brain. Often memories of traumatic events are stored in the portions which control how humans relate to their bodies.

Co-Awareness- An important step towards gaining control of one's life for a person living with DID is becoming co-aware. In this stage, all or most of the alters gain awareness of each other's feelings, emotions, and memories.

Co-Conscious- Being able to be present in as many situations as possible is extremely important to the waking self in a multiple system. Becoming co-conscious means that whenever an alter emerges, the waking self is aware and awake and thus able to be in on any decisions and actions the emerged alter might make.

Cognitive behavioral therapy (CBT)-a structured, action-oriented and problem-solving approach which helps people to manage their thoughts, behavior and mood more effectively.

Complex Post-Traumatic Stress Disorder- Children who suffer chronic trauma such as abuse and a disruption in attachment to their caregivers, may develop Complex Post-Traumatic Stress Disorder.

Co-Occurring Diagnosis- Often a person living with DID will have other disorders accompanying it such as borderline personality disorder or major depression.

Core- The central, sometimes original ego state of a multiple system.

Covert Switching- Changing from one alter to another without being noticed by people outside the person's system.

Crisis-Psychiatric crisis describes the situation where a person with a mental illness or severe mental disorder experiences thoughts, feelings or behaviors which cause severe distress to him/her and those around him/her.

Denial – a defense mechanism in which the existence of unpleasant internal realities is denied and kept out of conscious awareness. By keeping the stressors out of conscious awareness, they are prevented from causing anxiety. Denial can also be defined as telling oneself that an event either did not happen as they recalled it or that it did not happen at all.

Depersonalization- A detachment within the self, regarding one's mind or body, or being a detached observer of oneself.

Subjects feel they have changed and that the world has become vague, dreamlike, less real, or lacking in significance. It can be a disturbing experience.

Derealization- A persistent or recurring feeling of being detached from one's body or mental processes, like an outside observer of their life and/or a feeling of being detached from one's surroundings.

Depression-a normal emotion, which can lead to a very serious illness (often called major depression, clinical depression or depressive illness).

Dissociative Identity Disorder- According to the Diagnostic and Statistical Manual, 5th Addition, (DSM-5) a person must meet the following criteria to be diagnosed with Dissociative Identity Disorder:

1. Two or more distinct identities or personality states are present, each with its own relatively enduring pattern of perceiving, relating to and thinking about the environment and self.

2. Amnesia must occur, defined as gaps in the recall of everyday events, important personal information and/or traumatic events.

3. The person must be distressed by the disorder or have trouble functioning in one or more major life areas because of the disorder.

4. The disturbance is not part of normal cultural or religious practices.

5. The symptoms are not due to the direct physiological effects of a substance (such as blackouts or chaotic behavior during alcohol intoxication) or a general medical condition (such as complex partial seizures).

Dissociation- A mental process of disconnecting from one's thoughts, feelings, memories or sense of identity.

Dissociative Disorders – mental disorders that involve experiencing a disconnection and lack of continuity between thoughts, memories, surroundings, actions and identity. People with dissociative disorders escape reality in ways that are involuntary and unhealthy and cause problems with functioning in everyday life. Dissociative disorders usually develop as a reaction to trauma and help keep difficult memories at bay. Symptoms — ranging from amnesia to alternate identities — depend in part on the type of dissociative disorder you have. Times of stress can temporarily worsen symptoms, making them more obvious.
Dry Wells- People who have no emotional support to give.

DSM-V- The Diagnostic and Statistical Manual of Mental Disorders is published by the American Psychiatric Association and offers a common language and standard criteria for the classification of mental disorders

Eeyore Complex- A chronic depressed outlook on life where the person is always relating to others the negatives of their day to day life experiences.

False Memory Syndrome Foundation- A nonprofit organization founded in 1992 by Pamela and Peter Freyd, the FMFS purports to examine critically the concept of recovered memories, and supports the belief in false memory syndrome. https://www.fmsf.org

False Memory Syndrome- Described as a condition in which a person's identity and relationships are affected by memories that are factually inaccurate, but that they strongly believe. False memory syndrome is not a scientifically accepted or proven condition, nor is it found in the DSM-5.

Flashback- A reliving of an event of trauma as though the person were back in the time and place of the occurrence.

Fragment- A partial ego state, such as a nonverbal child.

Fugue- a psychological state in which a person loses awareness of their identity or other important autobiographical information and engages in some form of unexpected travel. People who experience a dissociative fugue may suddenly find themselves in a place, such as the beach or at work, with no memory of how they got there. Similarly, they may find themselves somewhere in their home, such as a closet or in the corner of a room, with no memory of going there.

Functional Magnetic Resonance Imaging (fMRI) - a device that measures brain activity by detecting changes associated with blood flow. This technique relies on the fact that cerebral blood flow and neuronal activation are coupled. When an area of the brain is in use, blood flow to that region also increases.

Generalized Anxiety Disorder (GAD) - a condition characterized by 6 months or more of chronic, exaggerated worry and tension that is unfounded or much more severe than the normal anxiety most people experience.

Hippocampus- The hippocampus is involved in the storage of long-term memory, which includes all past knowledge and experiences. The hippocampus seems to play a major role in declarative memory, the type of memory involving things that can be purposely recalled.

Hypersomnia- refers to either excessive daytime sleepiness or excessive time spent sleeping, is a condition in which a person has trouble staying awake during the day. People who have hypersomnia can fall asleep at any time -- for instance, at work or while they are driving. They may also have other **sleep**-related problems, including a lack of energy and trouble thinking clearly.

Insomnia- clinically defined as the 'inability to initiate or maintain sleep or to obtain good sleep quality despite adequate opportunity to do so, accompanied by significant daytime consequences of poor sleep' (American Academy of Sleep Medicine, 2005). It's worth noting that insomnia is highly subjective and individual sleep requirements vary considerably.

Integration- a highly controversial topic among people living with Dissociative Identity Disorder. Integration occurs when the ego states (alters) achieve their highest level of co-awareness, cooperation, and co-consciousness.

Major Depressive Disorder (MDD) – also clinical depression, this disorder affects how you feel, think and behave and can lead to a variety of emotional and physical problems. You may have trouble doing normal day-to-day activities, and sometimes you may feel as if life isn't worth living. More than just a bout of the blues, depression isn't a weakness and you can't simply "snap out" of it. Depression may require long-term treatment. But don't get discouraged. Most people with depression feel better with medication, psychotherapy or both.

MRI- Magnetic Resonance Imaging. It is a radiological test where a strong magnet is used to visualize soft tissues in the body. It is painless, but it can take a great deal of time to perform.

Multiple Personality Disorder- The old term for Dissociative Identity Disorder. Its name was changed in 1994.

Panic attack-sudden periods of intense anxiety which appear to have no obvious triggers or reasoning. They can happen when a person least expects it and can be very distressing and frightening for the sufferer.

Personality-This term refers to individual differences in characteristic patterns of thinking, feeling and behaving which are attributed to an individual. Our personalities begin to be formed before birth and continue to evolve until death.

Phobias-are characterized by feelings of fear or anxiety triggered by situations or objects.

Psychotherapy- Often referred to as "talk therapy", this psychological tool consists of a client sitting with a mental health professional and working out through exploring personal insights, the problems they feel they need help with

Relapse- Falling back into old patterns that one has determined to be negative to one's health and happiness.

Singleton- Anyone who does not experience the splitting (switching) which is the hallmark of dissociative identity disorder.

Somatic Symptom Disorder (SDD) – formerly known as "somatization disorder" or "somatoform disorder", this disorder is a form of mental illness that causes one or more bodily symptoms, including pain. The symptoms can involve one or more different organs and body systems, such as: Pain. Neurologic problems. Gastrointestinal complaints.

Splitting- Switching from one alter to another, it is also known as switching. Splitting is often out of the person living with DID's control.

Stress- An occurrence which causes a person to feel a heightened sense of alertness. There is always stress in our lives, however some stress is toxic in that it overwhelms our abilities to cope and drives us to do things to cope we would not normally do.

Stress Hormones- Our brains have a mechanism to ready us to respond to any perceived threat and stress hormones are a key to this response. When a threat is perceived, the hypothalamus (an organ located in the brain) to send signals to other parts of the body including the pituitary gland, which is responsible for secreting adrenocorticotropic hormone (ACTH). This hormone then forces the adrenal glands to produce the hormone corticosteroid to increase the body's readiness to flee, fight, or freeze to avoid or escape danger. These responses are automatic, and it is important to note that they are triggered by what the brain PERCEIVES as a threat, not necessarily the fact that a threat exists in the here and now.

Survivor- A person who has lived into adulthood after experiencing childhood trauma.

The prevalence of DID- in the general population of the United States is 1% (1 out of 100) afflicting around 3.2 million people. It is Schizophrenia which afflicts 3.5 million people in the US.

Therapist- A highly trained mental health professional who offers hope and help to persons in need of someone to speak with to overcome an adversity in their life.

Thriver - a happy, self-confident and productive individual who believes that she has a prosperous life ahead. She is primed to follow her dreams, go back to school, find a new job, start her own business or write her story.

Trigger- A trigger is something that sets off a memory, flashback or dissociative event. Triggers are very personal as different things trigger different people. They can involve all five of the senses and are very hard to avoid all the time.

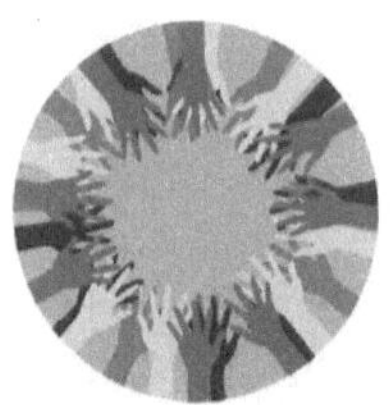

Resources to Find Help for Dissociative Identity Disorder

Online Support Groups:

Ivory Garden: https://www.igdid.org

FTASS: https://www.ftass.net

Find a Therapist Sites:

Psychology Today:

https://www.psychologytoday.com/us/therapist/dissociativedi
sorders

International Society for the Study of Trauma and Dissociation
(ISST-D):

https://www.isstd.connectedcommunity.org/network-
network-find-find-a-professional

Find a Psychologist:

https://www.findpsychologist.org